The Wake-Up Blast

by

Hall Gardner

Narcissus Press, New York

www.narcissuspublications.com

ISBN: 978-0-6152-1956-1

FIRST EDITION

Preface

The Wake-Up Blast represents over thirty years of poetic protest and dissent. The poems— set in urban and *sub-urban* locations throughout the planet— Paris, Madrid, Moscow, Beijing, Nanjing, Hong Kong, Bangkok, Ho Chi Minh City, Doha, Agadir, Carthage, Rio de Janeiro, NYC, Harlem, New Orleans, Washington, D.C.— not to overlook Wilmington, Delaware where I grew up— explore a wide range of explosive political and social themes generally from the perspective of personal encounters.

The poems of *The Wake-Up Blast* represent rallying cries against living in fear and violence; against the poisoning and destruction of the environment; against financial speculation and the burgeoning gap between rich and poor; against human rights abuses and torture; against the electric chair and death penalty; against all forms of gender, ethnic, racial and religious discrimination; against totalitarianism and state repression of autonomy and democracy movements; against the outrageous suffering of global refugees, the poor and the marginalized, of immigrants and minorities, and of innocent men, women and children in meaningless wars throughout the planet.

The Wake-Up Blast protests against the looming threat of perverse forms of militarism and "ethnic cleansing"; against the renewed build-up of nuclear and conventional weaponry and an arms rivalry now venturing into outer space; and against the real possibility of permanent world-wide—if not major power—conflict after those four riders of an Apocryphal Apocalypse struck the World Trade Center and Pentagon on September 11, 2001—attacks followed by the disastrous U.S.-led intervention in Iraq in March 2003 and the ongoing military build-up in the Persian Gulf, Indian Ocean, Far East and elsewhere.

In writing *engaged* poetry, my purpose is, on one level, political, that is, to take a stand against both war and the various hydra-headed forms of "terrorism"— as ways to resolve disputes and conflicts. The title poem— *The Wake-Up Blast*— represents a poetic protest against the March 11, 2004 massacre of passengers in the Madrid metro system, among other acts of anti-state and state-supported "terrorism" in the Middle East and throughout the world that appeared to accelerate in the wake of the September 11 attacks. The poem thus opposes violent extremism of *all* forms and calls out for peace wherever passions— particularly (but not exclusively) those expressed in the name of conflicting Apocalyptic visions— provoke acts of "terror" and "counter-terror."

On a deeper level, my intent is to interweave the often abstract and seemingly exterior issues of the social and political with the more intimate aesthetics and ethics of the personal. In the endeavor to interlink the personal with the social and the political through the medium of poetry, my hope is to engage the reader in a *counter-visionary* quest to transcend the present global crisis by way of discerning differing means to resolve disputes and conflicts of all kinds, yet without recourse to violence wherever possible.

The poems of *The Wake-Up Blast* are consequently for the ultimate goal of pluri-cultural tolerance and religious understanding; for respect for civil rights through inter-personal and consociational cooperation; for an end to poverty and suffering through power- and profit- sharing; for sustainable development, energy alternatives and an uncontaminated environment; for an end to daily violence, weapons rivalries and war; for truly *engaged* diplomacy; for justice through the process of reconciliation.

—Hall Gardner,

Paris, March 2008

For Isabella, Celina, Francesca, and Paprika;
For those who played a part in this creation;
For Diana and Bill who brought these poems
out of the shadows and into the light...

The Wake-Up Blast

Table of Contents

There are no stirrups:
The poet must ride bareback.

Sub-Urban Landscape

Upon the backs of horses
across oceans these houseflies sailed.

Not native to this clover
honey bees ambush the toes of infants.

The creek evaporated:
Tadpoles no longer blossom into frogs.

Amid the sky— blue as a robin's egg—
gnats gyrate like electrons.

—1980

Sub-Way Map

Sub-

way

cars

black...

gray...

blue...

sting

the

colors

of

a

sweltering

bruise

X-ed

out

by

switchblade

the

Metro

map

no

longer

guides

us

LOST

long

past

our

stop

—1983

Splinters the Length of Daggers

"The air is so crowded with *keres*: there is not one empty chink into which you could push the spike of a blade of corn." —Anonymous Greek Poet

Splinters the length of daggers...
Tinted fragments of glass
as razor sharp as the teeth
of these cattle and sheep
which graze upon these
Harrisburg herbs...

These images pierce
the inflamed heart of my body
which I offer as a Geiger counter
to search through ancient valleys
for a presence... *invisible...*

that had once seeped
into creatures become fossils,
and that now creeps
into the eerie groundswell
of our spirit...

become
a canary
trembling...

lowered
cautiously
into a mineshaft,
deeper
and deeper...

Though sleepless I cannot cease my exploration:

I stare... *incredulous...* at the hues
of a child's disfigured limbs
jagged as the bones of a trilobite
embedded in shale...
scorched by the sun.

I am baffled utterly
by the atrophied sinews
of our inhumanity
as they coruscate
upon the sliding board
of this evacuated playground:

The awkward gait,
the slow silent step
into the next oblivion,
each having spelunked
out of murky... *unfathomable...*
caverns
of our intimate passion
within the ebb and flow
of the Love Canal...

There— toxic!!!
There— infertile!!!
There— mutant!!!
There— sterile!!!

The earth quakes
beneath the chaff of this grass
beneath the trails of thistles and thorn patches
beneath newly arisen vines
that ensnare these wild roses
whose delicate vermilion heads
are to be decapitated by humans for humans
to rest their skeletal residues.

Barefoot I step into the clover
now pollinated by sperm
transported by bees....

—1979

A *Sub-Urban* Holocaust

"Currently, the U.S. has three reactors at Savannah River, S.C., operating at two-thirds of their capacities, turning out weapons-grade plutonium and tritium for the biggest weapons-building program the country has undertaken in 20 years."

—*Washington Post* (May 5, 1980)

His hair was flaming orange,
that innocent boy we used to tease.
Everyone pushed him around.
Rarely did he talk back. So serene.
Even when the baseball
cracked his front teeth.

His father... *somber*... worked
in the garden the day long.
Mowed the grass. Well respected by all.
Suburban. Very *sub-urban.*
There was absolutely no reason
for me to suspect.

Beneath the Stagg field squash court,
where a labor strike had shifted
the project from the Argonne forest
into the city of Chicago itself,
his father had worked... diligent... *hush-hush....*
No one would suspect.

With its Calutrons wrapped
like dental braces with silver wires
borrowed from the Treasury,
fears that the radioactive mass
might accidentally go critical
were peremptorily dismissed.

With the hog butcher of the world
diligently inspecting shipments
of K-rations for the brave troops overseas:
No one would have ever realized *if...*

The blow had been something much more
than a mere crack in his teeth...

THE VERY JAWS OF HIS SKULL
SPLIT APART BY A SCRAP OF METEORITE
AND HIS ORANGE HAIR BEGAN
TO BURN UPON HIS BLOOD SCALP

THE WHOLE EARTH STAGGERED
AS IF IN AN EPILEPTIC FIT
AND SWALLOWED WHOLE THE FURY
OF ITS BABBLING TONGUES

THE SUN ITSELF PLUMMETTED
TO THE METALLIC SANDS
AND ENGRAVED HIS SHADOW
INTO THE CEMETARY STONE

LEPEROUS FLESH WAS RESURRECTED
FROM ITS ANCIENT TOMB
AND DRIPPED LIKE MOLTEN LAVA
FROM HIS GUILT-RIDDEN BONES.

EVEN THE RIVERS COULD NOT
COOL HIS FLAMING HAIR
IN THE AWESOME SERENITY
THAT OVERWHELMED HIM...

Upon my return, I was witness
to the blaze of his hair
upon the *sub-urban* lawn,
smoldering without attention.

It was Sunday. Certainly no one
suspected the embers to spread,
certainly not he who was
on leave after working...

So *diligent*... like his father
who was standing... *so somber*... before him...
in the service of Pluto, Mars,
and Fission Incorporated.

As he approached, I feared the emanations
from the touch of his palm...

—Why the hell did you decide to work there???
I wish you would quit!!!

"If I wasn't there to supervise, I know for
sure somebody else would."

—But don't you fear for yourself?
Don't you fear to be exposed???

"The badge warns us, but the dust
does spread on the hands and the feet."

—And what about the workers, aren't they exposed
even more than you?

"Hell, that's what they're paid for,"
he quipped without concern,
"That's what they're paid for."

Still haunted by his serene composure,
I must declare:

Has the Breeding of a Nuclear Holocaust become—

A Family Affair???

—1978/1983

Interpreter

(for Isabel)

Blackberries scamper like caterpillars across the pavement as I enter this residential palace. Interpreter between two warring factions, I am to pronounce... cautiously... graciously... the implied threats muttered beneath the cocktail breath of diplomats.

Caught in the crossfire, I must raise a white flag. I stand accused of rekindling the flames: My choice of words too acerbic, not chosen subtly enough to please the wakeful ears of those who pretend to hear nothing but who are yet everywhere listening [to the slightest twist of the wrist, twitch of the eye]— and who spy out each tidbit of fraud trapped beneath a forked tongue.

I must speak of [Armageddon] with a clever wit as if I am reporting some sporting event... detailing the sides... the batting average... the coaching tactics... the pitcher's skill... the win-loss record... the ratio of kill to over-kill.

Here blackberries lie [squashed] where these diplomats once stood. The winds allowed no escape. I rejoice for those who remain whole, whose fat bellies roll free beneath the willow lashing blindly in the night sky alit by the Molotov flames of cocktail promises.

—1983

"U'd Be Pushin' Pulp at the Pentagon"

Here, unleashed from the eternally locked vault
at the South Dock of the Pentagon Parking Lot,
lie the bared essence of every classified document,
every conniving Contra-Iran/Iraq-type plot
and *coup d'etat*; every kickback, pay-off,
and overpriced spare part, and every tidbit
of bedroom and girlie data compiled on political
and not-so-political dissidents and suspects.

All Man&Womankind Would Just Wet
its Pants for this Disclosure!!!

Just like the Moscow embassy, the guard's takin'
a break at the snack bar. Almost as easy as praisin'
the Pope, but then breakin' into the Vatican archives,
I need only jump out and devour every scandal
now key-punched on a computer processing card.
Yeah, I, world-renown temporary employee
of General Recycling will pledge (scout's honor)
to scout out all unprocessed elements of classified pulp.
All secrets (thoroughly gobbled in a washer and
vomited onto a conveyor), I will pile five feet deep
in a Mack truck trailer by shovel to be recycled
in New Jersey for the Generals to recycle once again.

—1979; 1986

A Georgetown Wake

I.

August is like lurking in the dizziness of a tunnel—watching the myriad refractions of traffic passing, fainting without oxygen mask. Rocky streets, which once meandered like evaporated streams before the days of the horseless carriage, are now paved over by macadam. Trolley car tracks rust as mementos long forgotten.

The haze envelops the brownstone edifices: The insignificance of gray casts an opiate cloud of impotence. Children slap one another in futile brawls. Single women hide their inner bruises with a ghoulish mauve spread upon their cheekbones. It is the latest fashion. With their eyes on the outlook, young men pace beneath willows weeping alone.

What life is there in the loneliness of those trees, still strong and supple, which tower high above the inanity of our daily gossip? Can the blind limbs of vines that stretch out in uncertainty to the iron bars of my window sill still be assured of the morn to replenish their being?

II.

In the outdoor cafés waiters, waitresses are forever waiting... waiting. Oblivious, Georgetowners chat the French of the Tsars, mocked by roving bands of Black youth who break dance to blaring beat boxes.

On the corner, wizened hippies finalize drug deals, "Low prices to keep you high, man!" Rock and roll groupies smash beer bottles and flirt their marijuana liberties. Punk rockers puncture belly buttons and chain themselves together in the newest sado-macho fad.

Outside the folk-rock café, the street busker, after wailing "Mr. Tambourine Man," captures neither the spectators' hearts nor their wallets. The homeless woman begs the crowd to invest in her child's welfare.

The street musicians and magicians count their evening's revenues; flower peddlers and other street vendors, licensed and unlicensed, pack their wares once the late night parade of window shoppers and bar hoppers has exited. The hefty Black man, towering high above the crowd, inflates a giant psychedelic balloon with helium and calls out in a resonate Armstrong voice, "Make the children happy!"

Having striven diligently all evening to convince the clientele of the authenticity of their *haute cuisine,* owners of French restaurants— French nationals or *pieds-noirs* from Morocco, Tunisia— or even Greek-Americans— quickly close up shop, then race to their *amours.*

No Metro passes here for fear of upsetting the preservation of historic sites and the delicate harmony of nature, for fear, that is, of the letting too much of the "rift raft" from the "other side of town" drift down the canal.

As if in slow motion, a chauffeur-driven limo passes by. An elderly man with owlish eyebrows sits in the back seat fully illuminated by reading lamp, contemplating a book. The geography of the entire globe is etched upon the bulbous orb of his glowing white forehead. He considers his next game plan— with a mere flick of an eyelash.

This is Georgetown, empty, open, bare-assed, without its jet set discothèques of electrified clef notes ricocheting like shot gun slugs, without its dynamic diplomats and international crowd seeking the perfect or not-so-perfect Mister or Miss America.

As I trace the ashen shadows of trees, the air thrives with the air-conditioned love-tunes that cushion the dreams of brownstone trustees.

III.

Entering my efficiency, I commence my nightly ritual of sacrificing cockroaches upon the kitchen altar. The smoke from a saucepan of burnt spaghetti has sent hundreds scampering across the painted-chipped walls.

Beneath the prose of a starless heaven, I tremble for the returned grace of my Muse. I want to believe with all my heart that Jesus, Moses, Mohammed, Zoroaster, Buddha or Lao Tze will soon transfuse their spirits into mine and then fill my tank with the essence of their Spiritual Oligopoly.

Yet in reaching out for the beauty of those crimson specters at the farthest reaches of the aurora— in the quest for purely stratospheric inspiration— both Truth and Beauty seem as ephemeral as Shelley's multi-colored dome and the plastic fantasia at the local head shop: I find nothing but myself— a mere hungover angel without homeward direction stumbling upon concrete turf.

Vines grasp the kitchen utensils scattered upon my table; I cannot sleep within this August fever. Once again, I walk out alone to the moat of this citadel, passing the raccoons that nightly peruse the opulence of shopping bags tossed carelessly in the garbage.

Beneath the trestle that passes over the Potomac as it glistens in slow gurgling motion, white sailboats rest from their weekend voyage. Rainwater from the flash floods of the previous month rests fetid on the insides of abandoned tires, a perfect breeding ground for [*keres*]. Sewer rats have discovered their own amusement park beside the vast expanse of construction. Playful, they tumble like children; then finding a scrap of meat, they devour one another in envy.

I await, in silence, the thunderous resurrection of storm, but hear only the discordant shrieks of the earth's corpse as it shivers upon entering rigor mortis.

—1979

Sestina: *Agressão dos Cachorros*

"Damn it all! All this our South stinks Peace!"

—Ezra Pound, Sestina Altaforte.

Hark ye! A Sestina for the Virtuoso! Slanted Eyes attack the Garage! Ring the Cry for battle! Sub-Urbans unite! You've nothing to lose but your garbage! (Old Ezra resurrected a man just like this one from Dante's Inferno. Do I dare judge? You bet I do!)

Damn it all, John! Help rid me of this gobbledygook!
These mangy curs attack with devious eyes—
I say to the garbage pails and stand!
Defend our driveways! Onward— to the garage!!!
Hungry canines get out of hand; search for refuse,
then they defecate and spoil the land.

Do you wish litter tossed across your land?
Nay! So cease your saintly babbles. Don't refuse!
Our window-peering damsels are distressed; the garage
isn't a moat for canisters of gobbledygook.
The lids make perfect shields! Lance their eyes!
Dread not their cries! Damn you John— you *must* stand!

Yeah I hear— the malted Clouds— almighty they stand
above pasteboard barracks on treeless land;
but no Holy Deluge will ever scour this gobbledygook.
Show strength in battle! No reason to refuse!
Your shadow skulks 'neath my jeep in my garage:
Don't fear the Clouds' Wrath or dogs' metallic eyes!

Upon their gray scatological skulls, their eyes
plot yet another crusade 'gainst my garage.
Look! The carnal menace now huddles on your land;
the bastards sniff dappled bitches where they stand.
My innocent child detests such scents of gobbledygook
and the Heavens— wherefore an Answer do you refuse?!?!

No Answer! Out the poop scoop! Damn refuse!
Grrr! Even more intrude! More piles of gobbledygook!
John— how can you still trust their slanted eyes?!?!
These dust devils bluster 'cross your land,
their teeth yank trash while you decline to stand:
How dare you smirk when their Fury skips your garage!

Hah! Curs, fangs agape, now turn and raid your garage!
Hah! These mutts torment whether you seek Peace or Stand!
Like a slug you ought to suck your toppled refuse:
Yeah, let's fight— you Caca-face with peacenik eyes!
I need a good brawl; my soul abhors cacophonous land!
Combat we must— To spite all this gobbledygook!

Sub-urbans, canines all Stand outside the Garage.
Ezra's meta-physics Refuse amnesty to bloodshot Eyes:
Seems Gobbledygook may for alway lay flush with the Land.

—1972

Your Stepmother Calls You *"Pussy"*

You flick that long unkempt hair back to your ears.
The more you sweep, the more the dirt swirls
about your nostrils.

These grand houses cost more than you could ever dream.
With one blow you smack your fist through the drywall.

You watch the dozers tear down the trees
and uproot the earth;
your own home reeks the omnipresent fart
from the factories.

No presents for Christmas
no presents for your birthday,
wild man, gibbon face,
your friends call you *"The Chin,"*
your stepmother calls you *"Pussy."*

And even though they also call you *"queer,"*
you still wouldn't go whoring
with the other shit workers.

The wheezing raspberry-faced insulation man
asked *"if you jerked off instead."*

You merely shook your head and quipped,
"What are you guys so messed up about, anyway?!"

One day the Boss zips up in his Cadillac
and he surveys the ground
and he whispers to the supervisor.
Then he's vanished like a phantom.

"The Boss— he don't get laid off—
what's he got to worry about?!
He just walk in, say his NAME
and they give him food;
I walk in, say my name,
and they don't give me food!"

The carpenters, the painters, the roofers,
jeer with rolling eyes before you:

"Hey, what's ya so upset about?"

"Didn't ya hear? The Boss just swoop
down from the moon and laid him off."

"No— not really! Is it real?"

"Yep! I hears the boss lays 'em off one by one.
They says he ain't got no underwear
and he's ready to buzz at any second."

—1980

Brainstorm

The concept of the electric chair developed, at least in part, out of the debate between Thomas Edison and George Westinghouse over the relative hazards of AC (Westinghouse) versus DC (Edison).... At the time, reformers considered electrocution a "clean," "progressive" and "civilized" way of carrying out the death penalty.

All is so serene

before

the hurricane brewing

upon the azure

horizon...

My teeth grit and await:

Yahweh or Allah's bolt of wrath—
Zeus or Thor's bolt of whimsy—
Zen Buddhist Enlightenment—
Hannibal's grace of Ba'al—
Benjamin Franklin's key and kite—
Frankenstein's Awakening—
Kemler's Electric City of the Future—
Lenin's "Socialism: It's the Soviets plus electricity"—
Nicola Tesla's high voltage ray gun—
Hitler's Blitzkrieg—
The toggles of Milgram's $4.50/ hour "teachers"—
Phil Och's "Iron Lady"—
The leather straps of Warhol's vacant hot seat—

Ol' Sparky smelts
my warts
into charcoal,
my body
burned
at the stake
peppered
by gun powder
blast
barbequed
by the flames
of a yellow press...

The click of
the executioner's
tongue
now echoes
through
the hollow
of my throat:

Alternating Current
Is Definitely
More Civilized
Than Direct!!!

—1978; 2006

Taste of the Town

Not a smorgasbord
of international delicacies,
nor a buffet
of intricate delights.

Not a swimming pool
of fantasies,
nor jazz beneath
a cool September night.

No!

Is, in fact, the titanium
of slaughtering knives,
the toxic gravy sizzling
upon the reactor's core.

Is the gristle and sinews
severed from a human filet,
the pinpoint accuracy
of a vampire's stealthy sonar.

Is a taste of the town,
a taste of Washington.

—1981; 2003

Random Bullets

(13th and Monroe, Washington, D.C.)

Gesticulating wildly,
a woman swings her shovel
at the cursing traffic.

X-2's and 42's run their daily route.

Early Sunday morn they wade for hours
through a bog of cracked concrete.
As if waiting to kneel before the confessional,
the line is sometimes two blocks of silence.

Each prays for his or her share
of those little white wafers.

Leash taut— two Barzois more than half his size—
pull their master along the sidewalk.
These are not Tsarist gaming grounds.

A garbage sack floats like a dirigible
into the back black alleyway:

Hiding
their blindness
behind
his/hers
Ray Charles
sun glasses
the bean thin
couple
divide
the loot...

A lady ports
pink curlers
and black chiffon
evening dress,
her neck haloed
by a golden
chain store necklace.
She snacks (walking)
out of her
brown paper bag...
Her good luck gap teeth
protect her from attack.

The ex-marine tells his story: Jumped
from behind, stabbed in the shoulder, he
"Grabbed one by's de balls and smacked
his elbow right square in de nose of the udder."

A squash plant creeps around his muscular thigh.

A wheel chair crosses
the street before
the makeshift Cross
and empty flower pot
that mark the spot
of a previous
shooting.

His two bodyguards look anxiously in all directions.
A "No Hand Gun" T-shirt is glued to his gnarled trunk.
Headphones rap music only he can understand.

That
night
another
bullet
chips
the
side-
walk.

Parking tickets pile high upon an abandoned auto.

—1987

Respect the Panther!!!

Your Siamese brains fight
to command your body from birth:
White robes dunked your head in the pond
with the sign of the Cross;
black masks beat you with thatched sticks
in a secret three-month rite in the sanctuary...

With your one head drowned, you've clearly
forgotten your Christian name;
your communal name, *Domga,*
redeemed and transformed...
Dom means 'to respect'; *Ga,* the suffix, means 'not':
Domga, as a child, you were *not*
to maintain blind respect for the elders.

Passage into manhood, the priests discarded the *'ga'*
from your name, adding the suffix, *'bélé'*.
Dom means 'to respect'; *bélé* means 'the Panther':
Dombélé— Truly you command
the respect due to the Panther!

In the *Anti-World* your father had wed five wives,
the names of your thirty-five brothers and sisters
far too numerous to remember in your village
where grain is still thrashed with the same toil
of the same scythe that White Bearded Father Time
uses to emaciate Soweto children...

My anti-self,
my photo-negative,
your skin smelted with pitch,
we cruise, voyeurs together,
the *sub-sub-urban* world of 14th and P streets
to witness the sale of far more black
than white pelts:

"Is you datin'?"
"What do you mean, *datin'*?"
Ah, you all knows wha' I mean!"
"No, not at all."
"Den ask you frien', he know."
"How could he know, how could I know—
what *You* mean...

Slave of the Trade Winds
Bones dragged from your homeland
stacked on wretched decks
left to bleach on the shoals

Slave of the Cotton Gin
Lungs breathe cotton bolls
of the gyrating greed
of an indifferent ogre

Slave of the Hammer
Bruised polluted muscles
produce the malignant tumor
of squandered wealth

Slave of the Screw
For you, these salt n' pepper shakers
are merely the heads and tails
of the same galvanized chemical bond!!!

Dombélé!!!

These people have been
white/blacklisted
white/blackmailed
white/blackballed
for far too long!!!

We must speak in the oblivion of the *Anti-World*
where white is ostracized for speaking to black
where black is ostracized for speaking to white
where I wear the deadly smile
of your people's mask of death,
where the urban trenches reek of your people slain,
where the living corpses
of unrelated clans cannot speak
where the black hole absorbs the light of the cosmos.

There— Your Charge of Anti-Matter
Explodes the Polarized World
With the Furor of the Panther!!!

—1978

Nouvelle Orleans

(for Ken)

I.

Fog solidifies into a Diesel truck:
Leaping from his nightmare
Trinidad's Poet grabs the wheel.

With cracker crumb eyes we nod off
into Alabama 4:00am truck stop:
Eyeballs beam like spotlights
from shotgun toting pick-ups.

Like deer in the brush
we drink from those fetid caffeine pools,
then stroll out—
Real cool... real cool...

II.

Our destination known
we have no need for maps:

We follow the tangelo moon
to where the great delta glows.

The river mouth opens wide
to swallow its succulence.

Across the bustling highway
armadillos scamper in fear.

III.
Southern pines
are not dressed in uniform
by these bayous.

Magnolias do not march
in stiff, pleated skirts.
Rather they sway

in long loose dresses,
branches celebrated with beads
of indigo and turquoise.

IV.
Booze-bored on Bourbon street.
Street-walkers hang thighs out
windows for sailors on leave
from Mark Twain tugboats.
Tom Sawyer is led astray
from devouring Pacman.

Red tassels blowin' in the wind,
Shriners test drive dragsters on freeways.
Street youth tap-dance for quarters
as in the *ante bellum* days.

Bonaparte was right
to take the money and run.

V.
We dine in a former cat house.

Questions perturb
the pleasant dinner conversation
of our cosmopolitan generation:

"If our speaking together
was once forbidden,
would our intercourse here
be forgiven?"

Out of the lagoon leap an unholy host
of creatures:
Scissors of jambalaya
worms of vermicelli
retentive anal mussels
the vulva of oysters
erect calamari...

Not to mention other insidious ghouls:
Chemical confederates
in white pointed hoods,
gas mask devotees
of the newly photogenic Klan,
come to pick dioxin balls
in the land of Delta blues...

It is too much.
We must escape
this accursed mockery
of sautéed polliwogs
and run
to the black, back alleyways
to the real streets
of jazz.

VI.

Poker face. Motionless. Not a word passes
from his lips. A chalk manikin porting
gold-rimmed glasses and cropped blonde curls.
I ask for a road map. He shakes his head NO.
Trinidad's Poet asks for a pressure gauge.
He lays it in his hand without a sound.
I ask for a rag to test the oil. The rag's
in my hand. It's up to us to fill the tank
in this full service station. The money's
in his hand. Expressionless. Deadly silence.
Even the sensual breath of pine cannot cool
flames of this countryside upon our departure.

—1980

Weep Harlem For Your King Is Dead!!!

This tequila morn
only we winos awake to breathe the petals
withered from a yellow rose...

So Plato condemned us—
my poet brother, not of my flesh,
your hands and feet shackled
beneath the pterodactyl wings of skyscraper shadows.

In the catarrh of blizzards I feel your suffering,
ancient as the many paths of *Ona,*
inscrutable as the Yoruba mysteries
of your chosen name,
and as street-wise as the Anglo-Saxon name
tattooed at birth upon your forearm
yet painstakingly etched out
by razors dipped in the acid rains.

> *Predestined: There is no room for Poets*
> *in this Empire.*

Once pen marks paper marked is our blood
mocked by the Republic
for whom a Poet is a poor, pathetic creature
who sprays the graffiti
of lies, revenge, rebellion, despair...
And in the belief of this Platonic lie

(and Plato, himself a poet, spread that lie),
we are blindfolded, thrown off bridges:

Either we, like Lorca, are blown away,
or else, like Adesanya, we...

Ade— your words cried out to us
and demanded that we shatter
the concrete that cements our feet
and then dive into the vibrant chords
of that river of jazz,
and though Harlem never taught you to swim
that day... *spontaneous...*
we would bask in the incandescent glory of the dawn
never again to be willing slaves...

Ade— your words danced upon the fire hydrants
and brown brick tenements of this Harlem
upon traffic jammed streets
where neither hearse nor ambulance can cross
where bricks and rocks are tossed upon the cars
of Narcs who raid the local shoe shine parlor—

A front for teenage junkies who snake down streets
porting plaid pajamas and the welts of their habits,
cattle brands of the slave market.

Ade— your words throbbed
in these school children's hearts
and probed far deeper than the needle
and its greasy spoon!!!

In this Harlem without your words
there is no rhyme
nor reason...
the pigeon cooing of portable beat boxes
whines within this taxi city
providing meager sustenance for this
un-
living
moment
to malnourished moment
never sure of the next:

You once told us how your father was blown away—
his cavernous skull
like a rat's skull
helicoptered to the heavens
by a street vulture
for not even a handful
of crumpled
dollars.

Asleep that same night of your roulette madness
(did you truly expect that chamber to explode?)
your son far away, far far away,
dreamt a bullet pierced his own palm
and a yellow rose blossomed
where rivulets of blood eroded the floor boards
like the torrent of a dam bursting.

He
saw himself like you
drowning
then buried alive,
the dirt shoveled upon his skull.
Screaming
he awoke his weeping mother
who could *not* console him:
"No— my son— your nightmare was not real."

We stand astonished
by the absurdity
of the push-button recording
of a three-gun salute
and sour army bugle
as it snorts taps
at your GI funeral
in honor of you serving
in the wrong place
at the wrong time
as always, in the wrong war...

And where the locust of tractors
buzzed in the background—
not at all like that *River of Jazz,*
that *Being-Jazz,*
that vital infusion of *Jazz*—
where we... *livid...* wept beside your casket
unable to witness the fierce glance
of your jaguar eyes,

our flowers wilted in disgust:
your grave was not even
prepared for you—

You who once painted yourself Indian red,
and then black as a Panther—
You who were always prancing in the heaven
of a Harlem rent party
and who would now prefer
to have been buried in a clown suit
than to be mimicked
by those Christian ministers
unable to utter the incantation
of your Yoruba name

Ade!
Adesanya!

Let alone utterly unable
to comprehend the fiery cadence
of your blasphemous words:

The protestation of a poet
crushed like an alley cat
beneath the skyscraper foundations
of the empire....

—1980

Lottery: *Life or Death*

(Three Decades before Iraq)

Well now, should he write a love sonnet tonight?
There he is, hunched over his desk, pen in hand,
sure felt an erotic rush of adrenaline, right?

She asked a poem; certainly he wants to comply;
yet seems his inspiration vacillates, fades... and...
to pretence a poem, undoubtedly a lie...

News headlines proclaim: "B-52 downed";
"POWs trapped"; "Smack sewn in GI coffins"
(stitched within their dried mutilated skins);
"Yippies protest naked"; "Nixon crowned."

His lottery number he'll learn next week.
With no desire to partake in international crime...
If only she could upright upset verse in time
and work to loosen knotted lines to speak!!!

—1972; 2003

Napalm Still Bursting in Air

During the very early morning of August 24, 1970, the New Year's Gang attempted to blow up the Army Math Research Center at the University of Wisconsin, which was believed to be developing secret new weaponry for use in Vietnam. While the perpetrators believed that no one would be present in the building at the time of the bombing (using 2000 pounds of ammonia nitrate), a graduate student was killed and three others were injured.

I.

Bell telephones clink for change.
Jeeps from abandoned U.S. army surplus
parade in circles beside rusty MIG's
readied for take-off...

From Ho Chi Minh City to Hanoi
the compartment fogs
back to the late '60s, early '70s...

Green rice paddies defoliate
before the Poet's eyes...
The bomb craters
of B-52s...

II.

Unlike those brave ones encased
beneath the *Red&White&Blue,*
then shipped off to Dover Air Force base,

her neighbor had 'fortunately'
returned home intact— yet
exercising in a wheel chair
with muscular arms— become
a no-legged gimp.

III.
A copy of her underground newspaper,
the *Heterodoxical Voice* blurts headlines
of the latest chemical company conspiracy:
Elephant farts intoxicate whole villages.

IV.
His curly hair,
his beaming know-it-all eyes
reveal such humanitarian
concern for the masses
on that "other side" of town.

He and his wild comrades
run their convertible roadster
onto the sidewalk.

Cigarette plumes
then snicker at the Poet...
unsuspecting...
who is forced to dive
into a rocky ditch
to save his neck.

V.
The television blares
the daily body counts.
The Poet's parents shriek
at the dinner table:

> *"Your father fought,*
> *your father's father fought*
> *and your father's father's father fought*
> *and your father's father's father's father fought*
> *and so you too will fight!"*

For the first time in his life
his dad smacks him across the jaw.
He runs back to his Poet's shelter.

VI.
Library books
are scattered
by a couple
of cherry bombs.
It's "duck and cover"
all over again—
as if practicing
those elementary school
air raid drills
[in case of nuclear war]
when school teachers snickered
at rounded butts of children
jutting in the air.

VII.
After Kent State
and the My Lai massacre,
and a million or so
Vietnamese slaughtered,
the New Years Gang
packed two thousand pounds
of ammonium nitrate
topped off with jet fuel
into a stolen van.

The potent blast damaged
twenty-six other buildings
but didn't come close to destroying
the Army Math Research Center—
the actual target accused of developing
top secret weaponry.
The explosion did, however, devastate
the more cosmic study
of superconductivity...

The overworked graduate student
was not supposed to be there...

VIII.
About a year later
her artisan bomb
exploded like Napalm
within her *sub-rented*
basement cellar.

Bloodied,
badly burnt,
partially deaf,
she survived
in handcuffs...

IX.
A decade later: The Poet
visits her former room,
planted neatly among
rows of *sub-urban* plots.

Photos of Phil Ochs
and Jefferson Airplane
fade disheveled upon the wall.

Got a Revolution...

X.
*Different strokes
for different folks*:

She's released
from years in prison
to drive a taxi over
the Bay Bridge and back

while he, captured
in California,
is released on parole
to attend law school.

Needless to say,
his Weatherman's
cigarette plume
no longer scoffs...

How far should one go,
how far can one go,
to protest one's country's
acts of immorality?

XI.
Another five years pass: it was then
that the Poet too felt that shock
when all that appears to be is not:
His mother, he knew, had been orphaned
as a teen in circumstances still unclear,
but so too, he now learns, his father...
just a few months after his birth...

So it is now in the name
of that eternal battle
of soldiers who can no longer
be buried... *unknown*...
and of the torches
of fathers fathers fathers
and more fathers
that are flaming for war...
that the Poet continues
to fabricate
his own scribbles
of dissent:

Meticulously
crafted
packaged
postmarked
time bombs:

Once unsealed
they explode
with the blast
of sunlight
through blinds
unraveled
and
fingers
outstretched.

—1987; 2008

Ho Ho Ho Chi Minh!!!

From waiter in Boston
to pharaoh in Hanoi,
Uncle Ho's portrait overlords
the National Bank.

For six Colt pistols
Ho (Code Name Lucius)
provided weather reports
for General Chenault.

Ho's men helped the OSS deer mission
hunt Flying Tigers shot down.
American penicillium (invented by a Frog)
is said to have saved his life.

After Fat Boy nuked the Nips
he read the Declaration of Independence
and Rights of Man, before the Frog's Guillotine
sought revenge (backed by greenbacks).

So solemn... we... march
into his mausoleum,
arms straight at our sides,
no fingers in the pockets.

Uncle Ho himself had wanted
to be cremated, ashes spread,
"No idolatrous monuments, please—
Instead plant trees."

His poet's arms folded,
he reads Dr. Spock
on the effects of war upon children.
Cold as M. Tussard wax.

Watching our every move
from the four corners
of his spot lit crypt: *Weathermen*
stand at strictest attention.

—1989

Saigon Dauphin

I.

Grass stained toes; white dresses hang straight to bare ankles. Two snake women approach. The one on the right rubs my arm with silken skin; on the left, the other blows a kiss. My camera, wallet, passport, vanish.

My head spins unable to take photos of the [!!!] as it unfolds. My guide, still smirking in forced friendliness, is commanded to hand me over to a hunch-backed rickshaw driver. Sporting a Yankee baseball cap, the dwarf spouts out orders to his flunkeys. Like a fighter pilot shot down, they lock me in a tiger cage, and parade me through the streets of Ho Chi Minh.

Only the name has changed. Bell telephones ring from deep within the 1960s. Signs point the way to the airport in English; we take the opposite route. The people babble and jeer... *incomprehensible...* as I pass through the open market of fresh fruit, dried squid, and plastic gadgets. *"It was a cancer that gnawed my bone since birth,"* I swear, *"not a V.C. booby trap."*

I am paraded before the guillotine of the Museum of War Crimes. They stop to take my photo beneath the wreckage of a U.S. fighter jet. In the adjacent building lies an enlarged photo, a pyramid of Cambodian skulls. Elementary school students in red scarves form a semi-circle around me and sing songs of victory. *"I only shot photos not people,"* I cry. *"Even so, our blood stained your prints,"* they reply.

A frail woman— a beauty of the old regime once married to a French fighter pilot— sells post cards and stamps on the street. A younger, more haggard woman weeps, exclaiming that I had willed her all my leftover possessions: my stereo, my clothes, most of my belongings. She had to sell them all to survive. A man with panther eyebrows approaches and whispers in my ear, *"I fight with you: Kill V.C."* and then disappears just as silently, still as deadly.

II.

My dauphin son sleeps somewhere on some park bench in the night, or in a tent down by the river, army cap and camouflage T-shirt, crew-cut— unlike the whole crew of rebellious American youth. A young man calls out to me in what broken English he knows, *"I American, You American. Same! Same!"* He has a picture of a U.S. army officer that looks nothing like me standing next to his wife; next to them, a Vietnamese maid. "This was my mother," he claims. I tell him that I do not know what he is talking about. He refuses to believe.

Almost identical sisters want to sell me their story, how their American lovers abandoned them, stones thrown at their children. They confess they've told the same story to journalist after journalist for a few *dong,* a few plates of rice. My pen, paper, camera, money, passport stolen, they pity me— I, who once boogalooed with one who looked much the same on a lusty stint in Saigon.

Others surround me; they are no longer very young men and women, dark-skinned and light. One with ghoulish freckles is wrapped like a mummy around the neck and forehead. He or she speaks English better than the rest— except for Raymond who raps with a Philadelphia slang. The rest look like any kid growing up in America, but with thin chopstick legs and arms... Not at all like my leg sturdier than bone— and that I have to take off so as to squeeze into position.

All promise to help me escape; and once I escape, I must fill out the red tape to help them make their escape, the sons and daughters of servants and bar girls, and spare-time girl friends and lost lovers. *"We've been waiting for you for fifteen years,"* they cry, *"fifteen whole years have passed and you no come!"*

No tinsel-town liberator: I am forever trapped within this tiger cage.

—1989

Khmer Confession

(Upon flying from Hanoi over Cambodia in a Vietnamese propeller craft while sitting next to a researcher who told me of the forced confessions he had found in Phnom Penh of foreigners tortured by the Khmer Rouge— just a week after another Vietnamese plane had crashed a few miles before the Bangkok International Airport after cutting back on fuel.)

We waved goodbye to coconut trees, waterside side cafes of Koh Samed, and set sail across the rolling aqua waves of the Bay of Thailand. For several days of clear sailing, we wined and dined: Hot and spicy Thai bass, Mae Khong whiskey, Thai stick sizzling.

Reminiscing those Bangkok nights, those wild streets with scents of ginger, jasmine, lemon grass and fresh basil, with a surplus of women like black pearls uncovered amidst the shoals of a deep-sea dive: Hours of traditional massage, then body massage in the surf of lather, panacea to all stiff-collar mid-life crisis hang-ups...

That shaved head German had said, *"they drive me krazeee— absolutely krazeee!"*... And then we toasted to our future, our return to San Francisco, back to our homes and families and wives and work, oblivious to the sharks that encircled our yacht, nicknamed Thai Haven.

We had no fear, no fear at all, as they boarded our vessel like pirates, jaws agape, broken teeth as sharp as bayonets. Forcing us to ground our yacht ashore, they took us to a small hotel; the sweat glistened beneath their red bandanas tied tightly to their foreheads.

At first they treated us well, fed us bread and water. With country hospitality we were welcomed, and as I lay down to sleep on a concrete floor, once again I dreamed of those wild simmering nights ...

The grotesque animal fornication of a couple banging [!] and [O] before a jeering and drunken crowd in Patpong— as if no one else was there, sweat gushing from their bodies...

The cherry red color of Betel nut chewed and spit into the gutter.... AAAAAAAHHHH!!!...

I was on that stage, an American spook, playing ping-pong with a dozen Khmer dancing girls sold into sex slavery by Chinese triads to Bangkok pimps....

—1989

Visiting the War Memorial

Monumento Nacional Aos Mortos Na II Guerra Mundial

—Rio de Janeiro

Watch as they march up and down the parapet,
bearing sparkling kitchen-clean bayonets.
Look! At strictest attention in space-man helmets,
marionettes strapped in the tightest armored belts,
stop... turn... salute the War Memorial once more—
as if goose stomping to some grand Wagnerian score.

Do you feel the hushed and lugubrious stillness?
Names of the dead rising on the monoliths, endless...
endless...

Regard the finely polished and speckled granite:
The monument is as austere as the sleekest rocket.
Its twin thin towers peak to the vapid sky
and connect awesomely at the summit by
a voluminous black metallic wing
which hovers contemptuously in mid-air it seems.

The shadows it casts are stealthily *creeping... creeping...*
and you know well that marionettes once cut loose
cast daggers *at whomever it is pleasing...*

"Isn't the sidewalk too long to this little spot?
Well, I guess, it is an impressive place to stop."
"Golly gee! This is a stupendous monument!
I'll go get my instant camera in just a moment!"
"Yeah, yeah, let's find a site, grab a bite to eat;
it's so so hot— I'm so sweaty and beat!"

How do you feel as your cousins, the tourists,
        come and go,
lording this venal funereal memorial show?

Shutters click at the blue sky's blueness,
at the sea and its cotton candy cloudiness.
Look as they look over cacti and bureaus far.
Look as they look gleefully
                        through the iron railing bars.

For there— spread out before these

World Souvenir Freaks

the *favela's* shanty tin and coffee crates reek
as if buried beneath the sewage grill of the pavement
and trampled upon by boots of marionettes
and heels of tourists' insentient amusement.

—1972

Jonestown Kool-Aid

(After the mass-murder-suicide of Jim Jones, demagogic leader of the People's Temple, and over nine hundred of his cult followers, in Guyana in November, 1978.)

Having commanded my priests
to take this final photo,
a picture more enchanting than nature itself,
a vision of a multitude of my lovers,
both fair and brown, of either sex,
flashes across the landscape in a brief instant,
and I am confounded
by the opulence of their trembling thighs...

To each Merman Mermaid
I offer myself willingly...
Let the poor, the suffering, the lonely,
Come unto me...
I offer the luscious milk of the Madonna
to the awaiting tongues
of kneeling apostles...

My thin saurian lips,
my basilisk's wry smile,
I can transmute the color of my skin
for I have descended from a race
of noble shaman and snake worshippers.

I praise the ancient ingenuity
of the boomerang—
Turning, pivoting, striking, returning
to the exact location where I once stood...

I shave my head leaving only
a locket dangling...
I wear saffron robes as proof
of my obsequious obeisance...
I delve deep into the skulls
of my followers
with stone chisels.

Breathing mantras of peace
I squat upon the jewels
of my people:
Quetzalcoatl reincarnate,
I return to the source of my birth
some two thousands years after my death
with white skin and the stout body of Cortez,
worthy of Keats' praise!

—1978

Canto por una Salvadoreña

Blown free in this land without mangos,
You teach me, the gringo, as you would teach a child,
las palabras of your tongue... *latino.*

Your gold-capped teeth flash
como estrellas en un cielo amenazador.

A night lily
far from
your family,
your beauty
reveals itself
within the cover
of darkness
then droops
when your
kitchen lover
runs off
with the bleached
rays of dawn.

Nothing has changed, you pretend,
then pull your skirt high up over your belly.

Confronted by the *maître d',*
you say, *"dos meses mas, señor."*

But you really mean, *"dos semanas mas."*

The *maître d'* just snickers
then turns cold as Spanish gazpacho:

"The owner doesn't want women with big bellies...
no quiere mujeres con barriga....
Your work here is finished: *tu trabajo ha terminado.*
A la casa, señora, a la casa. »

Staring vacantly into the fireplace,
you freeze and cannot respond...

How your schoolgirl eyes once wept
when armed men in black masks
gouged out the eyes of your teacher
before the eyes of the entire class.

How your school desk rattled in fear...

With these garnets of grenadine
I string a necklace
to guard you against all evil...

Let their beauty shine through
your sorrow a long way
from the tart succulence of *jacoté,*
the sweetness of *nancé...*

May this amulet radiant
radiate far beyond
the machete slashed fields
of Salvador...

Como estrellas en un cielo amenazador...
Como estrellas en un cielo amenazador...

—1983

Generalissimo:
May You Cower In Sheer Terror!!!

(Written after learning of the assassination
of Orlando Letelier on September 1976 on Sheridan Circle,
in Washington, D.C.)

You must shield your butcher's eyes
behind dark glasses: You who
most fear the rays of the sun's illumination.
Your face writhes with the fury of the Minotaur
(more of a visage of a beast than of a man)
as the World watches you spit... then jab...
the barbed lance of the matador
into the trembling heart of a lamb.

You who have so blithely resurrected
the ancient curse of snake worshippers;
You— high priest of a counterfeit cult,
orchestrator of sacrificial ceremonies,
haughty conquistador of innocent peoples:
Behind your scarred bullock neck
glistens the anaconda's cupric skin,
its flickering tongue and crushing grin.

You— the supplicant and sycophant
of the putrid gangrenous flesh
of swindled black market greenbacks:
How seductively you are infatuated
with the redolent and succulent songs
of the bilious bovines in trench coats!!!
O Eunuch of Gringos— the World knows you prod
your prey with a prick of electric prongs!!!

May you cower in sheer *Terror—*
O Torturer! O Executioner! O Asesino!!!—
For no shock therapies will eliminate
the apparitions that haunt your temple gates:

THE MANGLED FISTS OF VICTOR JARA
STILL MAN YOUR MINES AND FACTORIES!!!
THE PULSING BLOOD OF PABLO NERUDA
NOW FLOODS THE STREETS OF SANTIAGO!!!

—1979

Nights of ***Manifestation***

(for Isabel)

A canary chirps in its cage
in the paint-chipped reception.
The room clatters water pipes
in twelve-tone chords.

Vermin writhe
within bread crumbs
tossed beneath tin cans
drained of battery acid...

A wino waltzes with
the blue-lipped mauve mascara
ladies of the Parisian night.
His proposal, the joke of Pigalle.

Emerging from his hotel room,
with only a bent nail as a lock,
his unkempt shoulder length hair
blows in a Metro zephyr.

His mind swells with pills
encapsulated in billboards
that tan the color of carrots:

"*Même dans le Métro...*
***Vraiment la couleur naturelle!*"**

Sludge of Cahors
& Merguez & Camembert
clog his flatulent intestines.
His disheveled Van Gogh shoes
do not know which way to turn...

Rushing through corridors of FDR,
Cosette de Passy asks him in French,
and then repeats in perfect English,
"The way to *la Manif*?"

"*To the right or left*?" he queries.
"*Qu'est qu'il est bête, ce 'Ricain!*" she snarls...

***

At sunset a cast iron ball swings
from the rusted boom
of the wrecking crane...
The listless sky... shatters...

The Seine glistens ...
entre chien et loup
below the Pont d'Alma
in twilight.

Waves of *bateaux mouches.*
The megaphone blares a guided tour
through *les egouts de Paris...*
All flies and rats aboard!!!

***

The motorcyclist tumbles
to the pavement.
His red scarf wraps itself
around exhaust pipes

The black van burns rubber,
Papa H. and the story
of the butterfly and the tank:
The ambulance?

The very shock wave knocks...
Voices... of protest... to the streets!!!

***

The
golden
bust
of Eiffel
genuflects
before
his 300 meter
flag pole
ignoring
the protests
of Zola
Maupassant
Garnier
:
What had
made him
so con-
fidently
justify
the ways
of metal
to tourists
to man???
:
Having first
fought so bravely
to save the Leviathan
Lafayette finds he must
stand guard permanently
to protect *Le Champs de Mars*
from such fervent devotees!

***

The crowd panics before the fireworks celebrating the marriage of Marie Antoinette and the Dauphin... The arsenal looted, the Iron Mask re-emerges to open the gates of the Bastille...

Marching from left to right, Brisot calls for war... *La salope autri-chienne* was really the cause of it all... Ghosts of Danton and Robespierre walk without heads from the Mountain of Martyrs like Saint Denis before them...

Marx and Bakunin debate the future of the state... Lenin searches for libraries and returns home late to Rue Marie-Rose... High in the sky, he regards.... *la petite Etoile Rouge ...*

Chased by bayonet from Barcelona, Eric Blair, alias George Orwell, pretends to be a wealthy English tourist, then resurfaces in Paris:

"Unity of the Left? Quelle blague!
Tout le monde boit un gros rouge
qui tache!"

***

Barbeque escapades in Asian rice paddies finally fizzle out; nonetheless teenagers in red psychedelic bandanas leap over the guardrails, switchblades in hand.

Ho Chi Minh and Pol Pot have long left Rue Letelier— just a jog down from *l'Ecole Militaire.*

The African porting sun glasses in the Metro smokes an unlit cigarette, then crushes it out with his heel.

In silken mourning shawls a gypsy woman begs for change and slings her Seveso fetus across hunched shoulders.

Soldiers fire *contra la poesia...* The invisible man sings. Human odes are hung for bait upon copper lines strung across geotectonic plates.

Escaping the injections of the Siberian Inquisitor, the Kadet translates *Liberty* into artificial intelligence then testifies in Helsinki, after being tossed out of Tel Aviv for no longer porting a skullcap.

Greenbacks are packed like frankincense upon camels wincing in desert sands; the gas attendant swears that he never saw a dime.

A crumbling mineshaft, *Le Super-Phoenix* smolders in the ash. Wax wings meltdown in solar rays.

The Concorde is at its sonic peak. Fatigued suits snore. Scotch... Chablis... Champagne... Air France aftershave...

London... Paris... In Euro-patois: *"Merde so long zu übergehen the airport. Bin Ich no longer le Commercant Supranational?!"*

Titanium wings of a more mortal variety strafe the omnipresent rows of factory assembly lines where flame the turbines of fighter jets...

No, it is not a hallucination of Guernica!!!

***

They toast the putrefying orb
With vodka and cola,
the co-rival astro/cosmo-nauts,

their golden umbilical cords
streaming far behind them, loyally
mesmerized by ***Spectral Emanations!!!***

The Leviathan, with its iridescent
Red&White&Blue iris, pops its own steroids,
then leaps from out of the seas.

For its part, the Behemoth snarls
on the shoreline: Its neck pressed
against a self-sharpened saw blade.

In vain, their hunched horrific shoulders
feign a macho muscular façade in an effort
to woo ***das Herz*** of Lady Europa

who must first overthrow the flapping
black hats of the Caudillo before smelting
the Behemoth's Hammer and Sickle

only to find that She must then cope
in desperation with the Athenian-like
ever-meddling and timocratic Leviathan!!!

***

All night every night
hundreds of thousands march from
the Bastille to the Place de la Concorde:

Banners held high reveal
not-so-subtle shades of militancy.
With whom should they march?

With the *A's* with wild white hair
in black motorcycle jackets
singing *Amour Anarchie*,
mouths stuffed with orange peels?

Or those chanting priests
in blue working collars
who brandish little red
Soothe books?

"Frap! Frap! Frap!
Poum! Poum! Poum!
Guerre Populaire!!!"

Or waltzing tuxedos who choke
on maraschino cherries
and gauche caviar,
their fingers snagged
on the brittle thorns
of red... red... roses?

Or else Les Cocos?
Who trail behind the blaze
of which Red Star???

***

The blue whoops of the sirens. Paddy wagons race over cobblestone and barricade the cafés.

The gendarmes of Adolphe Thiers check the surging *Manif* and turn it away from the Place de Grève...

Blocks from the Commune's ragged army... cars sparkle... set aflame by arsons' hands like fireworks on the 14th of July.

Tourists tap toes to the pulsing beat of the *Internationale*, *"Hey honey, come look at the parade! Not Independence Day, is it?"*

A las cinco de la tarde, the garrote screws a fraction of an inch... the gypsy poet chokes blood...

The waxed paintbrush moustache smelts time, screeching... *"Democracia es Mierda!!!"*

Cosette's distant cousin is one of the Caudillo's several lottery winners... *C'est vraiment la lutte finale?*

***

Sand bags recede into the distance... Flares descend from the heavens... Plexiglas gladiators now stampede in a pincer movement from behind the nation's not-so-concordant razor blade...

With no fear of *la Matraque*... when the very *Earth& Skies & Seas* are mutating before our weeping eyes... tinsel guerrillas pummel plastic armor... then scatter and tumble... crying:

"Franco! Asesino!!!
Franco!!! Assassin!!!"

***

Sub-Urban Child
Cosette de Passy
saunter nonchalantly
down the alleyway,
to watch wisps
of mustard gas curl
like a myriad
of roving caterpillars
beneath the closing
glass doors of the café.

—1975 ; 2002

Li Bai(jiu)

Dancing around your tombstone,
they are all gathered by that same rock,
where your canoe tipped into the Yangtze
while chasing moonshine.

Following the footprints of your shadow,
I hold up my own cup of Li Bai*(jiu)*
and *gambei* to your immortal memory.
Those in red scarves do not join my toast.

Now the honorary afterlife
member of Alcoholics Anonymous
your buoyant spirit no longer drains the dregs
of that degenerate class of spirits

after hundreds of ranting teenyboppers
suddenly unearthed your tomb stone(d),
ripped off your silken cap and gown,
and cried "Down with Poets!"

As you have always kicked against
the current, you know well that the Yangtze
doesn't suffer from spiritual pollution,
but chokes with the real thing.

May my poems too defy these prosaic times,
yet without leaking so much drunken ink:
The moon, you, and your shadow
overshadow all!

—1989

Strange Fruit in China

Night of jackboots
motorcycles and sidecars.
A convoy of army trucks…

Hundreds take to the streets.

I hum the Billie Holiday blues:
Even in Cathay strange fruit
sway from the branches...

"Hoooo— hoooo— hoooo…."
Some chant the International,
"C'est la lutte finale!"

Others carry banners that read:
"Blacks must obey the Law"
or "Kill the Black Devils!"

Like a few dried mushrooms in a bowl
then mixed with hot water...
so too the crowd spews forth over the rim.

I am enveloped by the throng,
rugby players in the scrum,
hot sweat and garlic breath.

With the strange cries
of screech owls, the hoots
of righteous fists of harmony

gurgle from deep
within the Yellow River...
"Hoooo— hoooo— hoooo...."

Following us in the hundreds,
the crowd surges forward.
Sadistic Buddhas smirk at our folly.

This night in Nanjing
hei ren bai ren—
black men white men—

smear as mere
ink blots
onto rice paper.

—1989

Hong Kong New Year

(Wong Yok Shin Temple)

One by one they arrive
until they number in the thousands:

They pass through red gates
and cram breathless into the temple.
They bear baked chickens and ducks in plastic bags.
They port sweet wine and oranges and apples
spiked onto sticks.

The devout kneel upon newspaper bowing,
praying in obcisance.
Venders hawk peacock trinkets
and garish red, gold, green pinwheels
that spin in the thick smoke of incense.

They are beggars without legs pleading for change,
supplicants who pray for visas
and passports to good fortune...
now beneath the Big Bank looming,
its lucky 18 floors (almost) completed...

All seek the winning digits of the astral plane:

08/08/88…

The numbered joss sticks or silver coins
shake, shake, shake:
The year of the flaming dragon has slithered
into the year of the snake.

A thousand rattlesnakes hiss;
joss sticks clatter upon concrete.

Frantic, each searches
for the secret meaning
of the *I Ching*…

But only uncovering numbers
without lucky eights
that merely repeat themselves
in an indecipherable pattern…

Time after time without variation…

1.9.9.1.1.9.9.2.1.9.9.7.2.0.0.1.2.0.0.9.2.0.1.3.2.0.2.4.2.0.3.1.
1.9.9.1.1.9.9.2.1.9.9.7.2.0.0.1.2.0.0.9.2.0.1.3.2.0.2.4.2.0.3.1

—1989

Goddess of Tiananmen

I.

When I— you— abandoned that morning beside that great mausoleum, just a jog down from Kentucky Fried where a queue of much longer length now awaits in impatience, the pudgy man within the great glass case with embalmed flesh and a rotting ear was perhaps not entirely astonished at what he saw and (at least partially) heard.

That three DaDa artists splotched his great portrait with red paint could not have been that surprising. Now cleansed and rejuvenated, Mao's lips— still bleeding crimson like his Warhol portrait— continue to bless all who enter/exit those heavenly gates.

II.

It was on this square that the Dowager Empress had likewise plotted to crush you, along with all those Ocean Devils, who had flushed China's lungs with the smoke of poppy seeds in the name of "liberty."

In meditating within her great bell chariot, drawn by dark green dragon horses bearing green flags, she accused you, and others like you, of abandoning silk gowns and of plotting to make all of China wear Western suits and dresses.

She was certain that the entire silk industry would go under, its secrets once upon a time stolen by the Emperor

Justinian in the days of Byzantium, upon the advice of a few Christian Intelligence Agents, who then packed the silkworm eggs into a monk's walking cane stuffed with manure.

In her rage and jealousy, the Dowager Empress painted your face with white mercuric cream after first breaking and then binding your feet... *The clip/clop of such an exotic creature, almost extinct, could still, on extremely rare occasion, be heard upon your ancient streets...*

Her Righteous Fists of Harmony wreaked havoc before being pulverized by the cannons of the Big Nose coalition. Those same noble spirits then ransacked her summer palace.

III.

It would become one of history's great Kung Fu re-runs as Shi Lang, after defecting to the Manchus (if you can't beat them, join them!), battled it out against the Ming loyalist Zheng Cheng-gong (alias Koxinga) in a face off over the straits of Formosa— with Chinese masquerading as Japanese pirates, island cannibals and bloodsucking mosquitoes encircling them both— and where only a few dared brave the voyage for deer hide and horn, the most potent of aphrodisiacs...

Death encircles them with sweet incense. Koxinga's skull throbs with anger and revenge; hallucinations haunt him even when awake. He deals in silk, sugar and luxury goods in exchange for gunpowder, a merchant of war and contraband. He screams at his children and advisors after his father and brothers were executed in Peking and his Japanese mother assassinated.

With 300 ships and thousands of troops armed with pikes and emerald swords, a shower of flaming arrows alights the sky like the sun behind the flight of geese. It was the perfect battle for revenge: Shi Lang likewise burns in hatred to avenge himself against Koxinga who had his father, brother, and son murdered when Shi Lang had sold out to the Manchus. Shi Lang had vowed to annihilate Koxinga's guardians of the Pescadores and then walk "peacefully" onto Formosa.

Once Mao had finally seized the Dragon throne in his own battle with Chiang, he forced the latter, like Koxinga, off the mainland to that beautiful isle. It was then that brigades of chanting teenagers marched the streets, tore up grass, and made their class enemies wear dunce caps. They smashed all cornices of the past— although sparing the brittle feet of infant girls.

With both still claiming that beautiful isle, yellow and red conspired against you and left you for dead.

IV.

Is the Good Earth so oppressive that Qu Yuan felt forced to drown himself? The great poet and diplomat had merely warned his emperor that Qin Shi Huangdi (Mao's hero) would become an oppressor, once he had unified all of China by force. After fleeing from the Court, he spent his time wandering through the villages collecting folk tales, writing poems, and staring at the Face Reflection Well.

Graffiti, inspired by Qu Yuan's Cosmic Questions, is scrawled upon the tombstones of the defeated Kings of Chu:

Maniacal Kings all thrive on conquest:
Only once they relent will I be able to rest!

V.

Against the odds you came alive. For a brief instant your flesh shivered in the breeze of marchers and banners, their hands armed with only guitars.

In those glorious and festive months, red and black ants had shimmered upon your pedestal— O! Tiananmen goddess with raven hair!— your blue T-shirt and yellow bandana— tie dyed in a world that had previously aborted the birth of flower children... at least since those ancient days of Mo Ti and universal love....

The thousands carried their yellow and white banners aloft; their fearless faces exposed to a thousand satellite photos, worth much more than a thousand words. As they fasted, our plates of delicacies spun round and round, plum lips, tongue of sea cucumber, breasts of chicken and pine nut... spicy *dou fu*...

VI.

Yet then, without warning, the Dowager's Righteous Fists of Harmony were resurrected and struck once again; hazy eyes purple with confusion, the People's Army turned against the people.

The old red geezers believed the movement to be fueled by transistor radios, broadcasted by those Ocean Devils from the Kingdom of Rice for whom Chinese ways will always remain "inscrutable"— although never a mystery for the Chinese themselves...

Da Zi Bao— Big Character Posters— had forewarned:

A gloomy black curtain shrouds the sky:
The Dowager Empress has re-awakened
after a hundred year snooze.

VII.

Like he who inflames the people then runs to the hills, I— the Ocean Devil— the bearded barbarian— who professes nothing, yet confesses all— had to flee across those waters, burning my papyrus poems.

The depths of the Pacific now between us, I sent you pathetic letters never received, pored over in bright lights at midnight by postal inspectors.

It had been you who had taught me, *how to write your name...*

VIII.

Your neighbor of twenty years stamped you in bright red calligraphy: ***Enemy of the People!!!***

"It was for your own benefit," she added emphatically.

After raping you repeatedly with the barrel of a tank's gun turret, doctors and nurses in white gloves and black frame glasses reported on all that they have fantasized about your "strange behavior." From there they shipped you to pre-prepared hospital cots.

Like a child lost in America, I paste your picture on cereal boxes and milk cartons, and write your name on a thousand poems....

IX.

Despite the efforts of that river dolphin (a species near extinction), Qu Yuan never rose to the surface: Each year the Chinese people paddle Dragon boats to toss *zongzi,* dumplings of glutinous rice wrapped in bamboo leaves, into the waters to keep the sea dragons from devouring his spirit.

It is said that one day he will arise from the depths

with your hand in his ...

—1989

Long Before Hungary, Czechoslovakia, Poland or Afghanistan...

The statue of Alexandra
you painted in bright hues
of red
undulated
like
those lines of verse
that danced
upon the golden domes

of the church
shattering
skulls of the orthodox.

Before turned to stone
Alexandra's flaxen hair
beckoned
to no avail
shimmering
in the winds
like the slashed fields
of grain
beneath
a cloud
in faded overalls.

The flames of Liberty's torch:

Snuffed out.

Sickles rust

in the residues

of blizzards

and boot

prints

spike

the desolation

of tundra

and thaw

into the dung

of slaughtered

pigs.

"From each according to his...
To each according to...???"

So Lenin

embalmed

in his transparent

sarcophagus

had vowed.

The bleak voice
of choicelessness
drooped
to a whisper
and then
whimpered
like a puppy
awaiting
the return
of his
master...

Mayakovsky—
no longer
a true believer—
put
the revolver
to his poet's heart
and recoiled
in sheer horror
at the profuse
leeching
of his people's
wounds.

—1981

Red Squares (May 1, 1992)

I.

Fortress walls of the Kremlin thunder once again. Loudspeakers drone out the laughter of orphans dancing. Folk dancers, clowns posing for photos, bears dancing the *Lambada,* and Russian army jazz musicians: All fold up their tents.

Red flags wave beside the bus-barricaded Revolution Square. The thousands march, chanting *"Down with Yeltsin!"* Red banners embroidered in gold. Chests proudly port Five and Dime store medallions. Relics scrapped in the ash heap of Party annals.

Goo-goo eyed, *sub-urban* children now snap photos of St. Basil's Cathedral, then coo at the high and long step rhythm of the changing of the guard, *"Juri, where are you???"* Searching for their guide, Innocents Abroad brush aside Old Believers.

"Lenin should be buried along with the rest of you," Juri scowls. Looking for a fist fight, he regrets not being there the day the empire popped like a Zeppelin but somehow without dropping from the sky in flames.

His friends— defiant— stood up upon a tank, their photo immortalized. *"You're lucky to be on the winning side,"* I tell him, *"After Tiananmen, satellite images still tell a thousand words."*

A moment of silence. *"Lenin! Lenin! Lenin!"* the Old Believers shout.

But there is no transmigration of souls: The embalmed one declines the invitation of the Spanish tourist board to visit the Canary Islands.

His sarcophagus winces in grief: Upon the façade of the old Dumas he so detested, black letters in Russian and English blare in new *Newspeak, "Freedom Works!"*

The ceremony comes to a close. Old Believers file from the square, cursing Innocents Abroad. Knives darting from their eyeballs slash publicity desecrating such hallowed turf.

Before the former Karl Marx Metro stop, clarinets sway from out of the roaring twenties. Son of Fuehrer II clichés in stereophonic sound.

Autograph hunters supplicate before the gaze of a celluloid star. I buy his newspaper but foreswear his signature, my guilty fingertips now smudged with radioactive ink.

II.

I talk to the one man in the crowd who will respond in English.

Tall, aristocrat of the street, long white coat, a high school English teacher, he tells me in perfect English, "he just loves to talk to foreigners," he says (for a few dollars, it is understood)— and has corresponded with a "delightful" lady in Holland for many years.

His eyes never look directly at me.

Speaking Jabberwocky, we discuss the global ramifications of Humpty Dumpty's fall in front of the *Bolshoi* while *sub-urban* children collect Red Army souvenirs and haggle for scalped tickets (starting at twenty dollars, getting down to five, sometimes even less).

One young soldier is willing to sell his pants for a few greenbacks; my street guide tells me that, by the way, he also has caviar and army uniforms to sell.... As if on a fashion runway, *sub-urban* children then port their newfound khaki camouflage to *Swan Lake*— to the evident disdain of the audience.

Then, as he stares [   ] into the clouds, he tells me that his son just happens to be a fighter pilot in the Far East and has much to tell me— but he's not permitted to speak to foreigners, he adds.

Needless to say, I decline the invitation.

—1992

Sturgeon Gasp for Breath

I.
St. Petersburg jazz:
"I'll do the cookin' darlin'
I'll pay the rent;
I knows I've done you wrong."

Marx's wide lapels (Groucho's, not Karl's)
are once again the rage.

II.
Outside the cathedral
the throng tramples
over tomb stones.

It is the first
Easter ceremony since
the enamel of the empire decayed...

I trip over a red star tombstone,
which appeared to sprout from nowhere
like a 1950's gasoline pump,
"Trust the man who wears the Star,
the big, bright..."

Chants of the Orthodox...
Unearthly...

III.
Multiple Matriuska dolls.
Some screw open from the head of Yeltsin
down to that of Lenin.

Others screw open from the heads
of either Yeltsin or Gorbachev
down to a very tiny Marx.

It really all depends upon whom you blame.

IV.
If Moscow had been capitalist,
Kalishnikov— of revolutionary
AK-47 fame— would have been
at the top of the Fortune 500—
with a percentage on rifle sales,
posters and paraphernalia.
At least he now has many many
medallions to show for it.

V.

It's a heated disco medley in the street shops.

Items for sale dance in a frenzy in the same glass case: Shoes, belts, socks, cans of mackerel, hand-woven tea warmers, rabbit skin caps, boxes of Stroganov, Chinese acupuncture sets (with scalpels and tweezers), caviar, vodka, caviar, vodka, caviar, vodka... vodka, mackerel...

Such trash likewise covers Blok's grave.

VI.

The clock at the top of each stairway
ticks to a different rhythm.

The elevator door does not open
on either the third or seventh floors:

Khaki uniforms and red epaulettes
disappear behind rock music video screens.

Late at night windshields glow
an eerie green: *Nyet.* No vodka for sale.

Sturgeon gasp for breath.

—1992

Viking Chieftain

That early Sunday morning, his head splitting from some cheap Californian Chablis of an open poetry reading, the Poet stumbles out of bed to buy bubble water and aspirin and becomes an unsuspecting witness to a not-at-all ordinary street person whose brain is not-at-all deranged by sleepless nights, and who does not spout out his demons by slapping his palms against gargantuan blubber, his wild albino mane blowing in the breeze, muttering *incomprehensible...* It is rather an encounter with a stereotypical blue-eyed blonde, tall and muscular, in knee high leather boots, who is roaring out his goose stomping excoriations in language so grotesque, so unrepeatable, so malevolent...

"Cow-vards! Com-moon-eests! Nig-ga Loo-vers! Fist Fookin' Fags! Jur Day uv Joodge-ment iz cooming..."

As he clenches his fist across his chest, his stained brown boots stamp those hostile words into the muck. It was such a slurred accent that hung over, 'open poetry reading' infested ears could not quite pinpoint his country of origin at the same time that it was indeed a voice that seemed to have originated from deep within black forests filled with pines and wind beeches, and lorded over by eagles and evil spirits of a Grimm's fairy tale world ripped off by enterprising story tellers and movie makers— a voice in full possession of whatever those satanic senses might possess...

Parishioners hide in the atrium; the Poet trembles in fear behind a parked car. Behind him, a motorcycle gang roars up the one-way street, their bikes chopping up the church grounds, circling round and round as if forming a wagon barrier against bow and arrow attack. Their comrade's corpse, with that strange greenish tattoo of an oriental dancing girl, who appears to wink at all who regard, sketched up his back and shoulders, rots in the sidecar of their fearless leader's cycle.

The gang has already collected his remaining things and his faithful dog, with its wagging tail and panting tongue— and have sold all that what was of value for his funeral wake, providing drinks and drugs for all— as if he was truly their long forgotten hero, the Viking Hastein himself, *baptized, deceased, resurrected...*

From the back alley, a teenager, eyes bloodshot from crack, also babbles *incomprehensible*; she staggers forth and offers them all a joint. Looking circumspect, they nod and reflect, "Yes, a young chick for our comrade, the perfect sacrifice for he who had died in glory at such a ripe age that late night in feast and festivity..."

The gang then lifts an old couch from out of the alley and fashions a mock tent out of fabrics tossed in the gutter. Their comrade's faithful dog, neck now slashed with his master's own knife, is placed by his side. After passing a pipe and syringe, they float his serpent hued body upon the churchyard fountain.

Each recites in prayer,

"Tell him that I have done this,

yes, out of pure love for him."

Hamburger and chicken parts basted in sweet barbeque sauce over a fiery charcoal grill are placed upon plates with candles illuminating the afterlife... With the wings of humming birds, each member of the gang then takes on the girl in their newly erected tent, and repeats,

"Who among you has partied with him
will die in Valhalla with him."

Watching from the clouds above, like a bizarre god-monster of Hieronymus Bosch, with the body and head of a crocodile and with the wings of a swan, the Viking Hastein himself descends from no-where to take his turn drilling...

In her ears he too whispers sweet eschatological nothings at once apocalyptic and apocryphal....

"Tell him that I have done this,
yes, out of pure love for him."

After setting the fountain aflame with canisters of kerosine, she too is thrown into the moat and hoisted upward next to their slain comrade upon his funeral pyre.

She cries out as the flames encircle her,

"Who among you who has partied with me
will once again with me party in Valhalla!"

Beside the spirit of the Viking chieftain Hastein in the netherworld are now all the spirits of the martyrs who continue to whisper sweet nothings... *at once apocalyptic and apocryphal....*

—1990; 2008

Speculator

Infiltrated by microscopic pestilence capillaries pulse paramecium through my scars and a flood roars through underground caverns where to survive there is only drunken courage and a gambler's hope.

Whipped by flagellum, dizzily I spiral from El Dorado to El Dorado— from Bangkok, Manila, Jakarta, Seoul, Hong Kong and Beijing, then off to Brasilia and Moscow, on the way to Tokyo and New York— busily excavating each vein of fool's gold. Like the heads of hydra my worm-infested metaphors multiply to the infinity with each incision...

Bets backed by pyrite, I am soon prohibited from crossing the trip wire of Wall Street black jack tables. I become as envious as that gray haired Queen of Spades— once upon a time serenaded upon Venetian gondolas before playing the Wheel of Fortune at the former House of Wagner— *Numero due vince!!!*

Those had been her days of glory before she lost her entire fortune in the Monte Carlo craze... *pressed by the surging crowd, the excitement of slot machines whooping, the clinking of coins, the red lights flashing, the revolving heads of two minks swinging from her purse of black gold and recoiling in the billiard ball shock of encounter. Facelift after facelift, her taut visage has never been at peace with itself: A curly mane hides the long scar of a scalpel's fine incision...*

Unable to cast my dice, now banned from entering any casino, I drool in spite on the sidelines and through my binoculars spy upon those who cruise in sleek convertibles upon zigzag roads over mountain cliffs that reach high over yachts docked beside Mediterranean shoals. Like a Venetian *Doge* guffawing behind a white mask during those months of *Carnevale,* with its *fantastical* and bawdy delights, I witness drunken nights of inestimable luxury where even cinema tale princesses can ultimately tumble from grace...

Somewhere I must discover a metal detector to filter coins from the soil or else uncover a sunken treasure as vast as crude deposits. And if all else fails I shall lay rotten eggs upon poisonous snares in order to trap whatever foolish creature seeks sustenance. With a real sucker born every second, I shall waste no opportunities: Become a taxidermist I shall then splay their wriggling bodies, sell their musk to any buyer, and spice their flesh with java peppers— as hot as lava...

—1998/2008

Culture Shock [and Awe]

I.
A random check. I'm lucky number 10.
Mr. Customs Man asks the life or death questions
that so perturb the spirit of our Nation:

"Been to a farm, ranch, or pasture?
Bringing in fruits, insects, meat, wildlife products,
snails, soil, disease agents, or cell structures… ???"

Thrust upon the treadmill my travel bags
abruptly enter into a black box oblivion
of all-penetrating cosmic rays.

Quickly he unearths emerald flowerpots
looped neatly with silken ribbons filled
to the brim with Belgian sweets.

"Imagine our 'state of the art' noses
confusing sausage for Swiss chocolate!
and we spent megabucks!"

II.
Instruments of French classical musicians
have been denied entry by US customs.

NPR supplicates in its perennial telethon:
"Support Us! Vote right now with your phone!"

Potluck D.C. potholes have only deepened
after my many years as a make-believe Parisian.

III.

The gas station attendant
with goggle eyes
begins his interrogation
for no apparent reason:

"I seen ya' stoppin' by
for gas yesters... day.
Yu goin' zee op-po-sit way;
now ya goin' dis way.
Cou'ld you tell me
where yu goin'
whas yu doin'?
Travelin' sale man
Or wha'???"

My head spins with the fumes:
I see myself muffled
in a bright orange jumpsuit.

IV.
It is Sunday, May 11, 2003.
The choir in black and white
chant in solemn voices.
The politicians sing. I cannot.

The woman minister (this
was not possible in my day!) commands:
Open hymnals to Hymn 616...
Hail to the Lord's Anointed...

"He comes to break oppression,
to set the captive free,
to take away transgression
and rule in equity."

V.
Alongside the Union Jack and Italian tricolor,
"Oh say can you see" flaps before discount liquor stores
where the other *'bleu, blanc, rouge'* has simply vanished.

An English beer hall ditty had inspired Francis Scott
Key... *"And conquer we must when our cause it is just.*
And this be our motto: 'In God is our trust'"...

As America dons the Red Coat of Perfidious Albion,
the rifts of Hendrix's version have long been forgotten.
The refrain is *"Love It or Leave It"* — all over again.

VI.
Before 9/11, bearded "Students" so righteously
blew up giant Bamiyan Buddhas—
All in the ninety-nine names of 'Allah.'

After 9/11, the Pentagon looked askew
as Baghdad mafias pillaged many
of the most ancient treasures of Humanity.

"Shock and Awe" had been planned to a "T":
But the *ad hoc* peace for "four or five weeks" only—
All in the vainglorious name of "Democracy."

VII.

My departure imminent,
I unzip the inner lining
of my larger suitcase.

Waxed deli paper unwrapped,
out plummet two objects— thick
as sticks of dynamite.

After voyaging clandestine
that Christmas cruise to Casablanca,
Dakar, and then Barcelona,

two copper-toned *Chorizos*
infiltrated the country
with alien cultures,

having disguised themselves
in fuzzy beards
of *Red&White&Blue.*

—2003

Transport Craft

You remember how those giant
transport craft had once soared
one by one like eagles over your sandbox
where your model jets roared
missile strikes against tanks and toy soldiers.
You were not even born when
those Hercules C-130s had once landed
packed with aluminum cased coffins

draped in *Red&White&Blue...*
My poor cousin from the Blue Hen
state with its own Mason-Dixon line
(that so neatly divides the northern corporations
from southerners farming chickens),
you took the very first chance you could
to see the world after those evil Saracens
struck the WTC and Pentagon.

Now far from your Dover sand box
you play volleyball and soccer
with your fellow General Issue
next to shark-infested waters.
Some flew in from Af-ghan-*ee*-stan;
others got it easy in *Ku*-wait;
and like yourself, other warriors
are on weekend leave from *I-raq*.

"It's not so bad..." you start off affirmatively
"but there's really not too much
to do sometimes... not at all like
they say it is in the News."
You pause a bit, staring off
over the dunes; you've said exactly
what you've been told to say...
toes fidgeting in the sand nervously.

"Yeah, it's great to take a rest,
even if only for a couple of days, but
you ain't allowed no more 'dan two beers
per night!" Worse still, you've been granted
only one hour of shopping— transported
to a weird land where it's dangerous
to even glance at the flash of a woman's
eyes behind black shrouds hidden.

"At night… the latrine is a couple
 hundred feet from the barracks …
If ya' got ta' go, ya' got to take a flashlight
out to check for scorpions scamperin'
at your feet… but just lightin'
a match can make ya' a real
sittin' duck for snipers…"
(It would be a good several

months before the big bad News
began to murmur that kind of report…)
With a wistful smile you assert,
"You know I never dreamed
Dover to be so damn beautiful…
Had always wanted to get the hell out…
It's only six more months
before I'll be shipped back…"

—2005

In the [Killing] Field

There you are
on a TV documentary
telling a Congolese rebel
with a machine gun
in his monstrous hand
that the killing
must stop...

There you are
with a telephone
in your frail hand
being told by your
UN commander
that it is not your job
to interfere...

Here you are
speaking to the audience
with your mother in Sari
praying you were back
in the Big Apple
typing like
everybody else...

Here you are
nibbling carrots
talking face to face
with some wondering:
*['Is it possible
to make love
to a Saint???']*

—2006

Agadir: *Sureté Nationale*

Three decades ago, the cinema opened its doors for the late night show... The house was packed; the advertisements begin to reel... It was a sentimental love story set in a Berber village that told of an idyllic time long before the arrival of the French and Spanish... The ground all around the movie theatre began to quiver and quake... Totally absorbed in the movie, no one in the theatre knew what had come to pass... Mother Nature, much as Rome had destroyed Carthage, had ravaged Agadir... Only the cinema remained intact to watch the horror show that soon surrounded it...

Spread out upon a hand-woven placemat,
a 'Winnerschnitzel' (as written on the menu)
deep fries her pale flesh in Argan ointment
next to her new found Kaftan Kebab
in the midst of a multicultural menagerie.

An Almoravidian woman in acrylic leopard skin
and green pashmina Sharia shawl
injects ochre hennae in geometric salamander patterns
upon the squat iridium-glowing thighs
of a liposuctioned French bobonne.

Behind them, a convex husband and concave wife
with heads attached to yellow sports caskets
waddle side-by-side like dromedary and bactrian camels.
Their sterling money belts are connected by
tightened g-strings that slide beneath each crotch.

A gravy haired blue-jeaned ex-angel-hipped hipster
fondles an earthen toned shoeshine boy,
with black polish and wooden stand in hand.
In *hoch Deutsch,* the pre-teen cries out,
"Amerikanischer schweinhund!!!"

No need to actually go shopping:
silver pillboxes, bracelets, T-shirts, Argan oil, carpets—
whatever you like— magically float
above the sands and lapping waves before you...
Just tap: http://www.opensesame.com.

Even the Berber trinket salesmen
know the exact arrival and departure times
of *sub-urban* storm troopers.
(The Panzer, cannons blazing, had previously
failed to find a "place in the sun" in 1911).

A policeman sternly admonishes
a photo fanatic for taking snapshots of children
as they play with a deflated soccer ball
in a narrow alley way: *"Vous n'avez pas*
le droit de prendre des photos sans leur permission!"

The tourist pretends not to understand.
A question of *Sureté National,* the uniformed one
then curses all cameras and threatens a class action
fatwa against all World Souvenir Freaks...
The planet shakes with the tremors of the next earthquake...

—1999

Hard Sell Carthage Burning

I.
Young men of Carthage
stare from out of their sidewalk cafés
in the sweltering heat
bitter mint tea boiling in hands...
bitter eyes...

Tourists spit out shells of pistachios
and pits of Carthaginian dates
onto the top of Carthaginian ruins
beside the machine gun-studded Presidential palace.

Amateur spies pretend not to take photos.

II.
Carthaginian admirals once proudly
surveyed the entire Mediterranean,
Sicily, Sardinia, New Carthage in Spain.
After that first Punic defeat, Hannibal,
the beloved of Ba'al, sought revenge...

Had a few more soldiers and war elephants
survived the treacherous snows
of the Little Saint Bernard,
it is possible that Rome itself
might have been vanquished...

III.

The beach swelters, packed head to toe,
next to ancient Roman baths
before the cemetery where (it is claimed)
the noblest families once sacrificed
their first born to Ba'al and Tanit...

Or, was more likely those children
had faded much too early in health to blossom?
It seems the soil of Lies must be muddled with Truth
to justify the disgrace and saline annihilation
of nearly an entire civilization...

IV.

In the arching streets of Sidi Bou Saïd
where the Sufi mystic Abu Saïd once dwelled
chaste white houses with vibrant aqua shutters
and hand carved aqua blue doors daydream
over the gray green waves to scents of pine...

> *"A gold necklace, a very special present for your wife, come with me, I show you, no worry, nobody bites, you can't get a better deal, he sell you for $200, me just $150, look for real, the match will not melt it, I tell you just $100, my first sale, 18 karat, you see the mark, it is for real, I must make my first sale; for free, I add jasmine, you know jasmine..."*

The young hustler suddenly stops,

hurling questions [and insults]:

> *"What? No money? And in your pocket, what? A banana? And other pocket, what? A notebook? What? Not possible! Your money with your wife? Not possible!!! You take necklace and jasmine to her; a present just $50, just for your beautiful child and wife..."*

V.

The streets are empty... sweltering...
Mullahs pace the forty zones of the compass
and call the faithful to prayer:
The *qibla* points to the *Ka'abah*
in either flat or earth-rounded directions.
Pigeons crowd over latticework below.
The clouds puff out in all their glory...

Your eyes still fixed upon the Straits of Messina,
World Souvenir Freaks spread salt
onto your ancient wounds.

—1999

The Wake-Up Blast

After the death of Ignacio Sanchez Mejias, Lorca told a friend, *"It is like my own death, an apprenticeship for my own death. I feel an astonishing sense of calm. Perhaps because I had a premonition about what was to happen."*

The wake-up blast of her alarm clock
belatedly warns her of what she already knows.

She has already stripped the bed sheets
and showered with lime-scented soap.

She sprinkles salt and pepper on her *tortilla de jamon.*
She stirs spoonfuls of sugar into *café con leche.*

She nibbles on deep fried *churros.*
She chokes down freshly squeezed *jugo de naranja.*

The balmy winds of an early spring waft
through the white curtains of the open window.

A radio voice in bass tones announces the daily news.
She hardly listens. There is no news except

That it is now 07:30. She knows she must catch
the train. She knows she cannot be late once again.

A pigeon flies up and flaps its gunpowder wings
into her face. On its leash a muzzled Doberman snarls.

A rat scurries from the gutter. Still she rushes onwards
up the stairs to the platform where the crowd

is already swarming. There she must jam into already
overcrowded wagons where she will be pushed and

shoved, obliged to breathe bull sweat and garlic breath
nostril to nostril— as on every workday morning.

A cell phone rings: A handsome man with a goatee
has a rendezvous *a las cinco en punto de la tarde.* For

a second, she feared her own office was calling. But this
morning she awoke before the alarm had even rung:

It had not let her linger in the breezes of unanticipated
rays and then let her make the usual excuses...

Arsenic balls and smoke cover the tracks at Atocha.
Death had decided to set its alarm at precisely 07:39.

The wounds were burning like stars at El Pozo.
Death had decided to set its alarm at precisely 07:41.

The train cars became coffins at Santa Eugenia.
Death had set its mobile alarm at precisely 07:42.

From a distance Death spread its gangrene on March 11:
Those horrific mornings of September and March 11!!!

—2004

Wheezings...

Piled deep in the throat
of filing cabinets,
mucous forms are coughed up
and regenerate
when typed upon a solution
of agar.

The pages sneeze
phlegm surreptitiously
once mildewed
by the soothing breezes
of an air conditioned
draft...

Yet even before the orders are stamped,
toy soldiers (not made of clay)
cheered on by Legionnaires
voluntarily march forth to battle
swelling erubescent ...

The word processing screen
goes absolutely haywire:
virus-loaded virilia (equipped
with earth penetration aides)
are programmed to be launched
from hardened silos...

Count down:

3
2
1...

Circular
T/
Error
Probability???

—1980; 2008

Who Dare Stand Against the Fissionable Glitch of an Eclipsed Fuse???

Caterpillar larvae burrow deep into their tent-like nests within the scarred skeletons of trees. Their antler limbs, as if hacked off by machete, crash upon parked cars. Scattered by sudden squall, the exiled exhaust of frenzied humans metamorphoses into muck fit for the fertilization of roaches beneath the nervous intensity of street lamps.

From the stratosphere, we peer down upon the cities flaming with the mephitic implosions of train derailments. As if celebrating Mardi Gras, we parade in the heavens in inflated plastic garbage bags like those fondled each night by the incisors of raccoons and bound tight by the elastic straps of addicts. Already fractured by the relentless incisions of razor wielding street gangs, the lopsided planet winds itself through a murky void of boiling oil and metallic filings.

With great striving, tarred and feathered, we attempt to scour clean our prickly spirits so that we, untarnished, may catapult in imaginary space vessels to the beatific realm of poppies and drones, but are left solitary to scavenge for what remains of the manna of twilight. Knowing all flights of fancy are heartily condoned by our philanthropic patrons, we still seek a reward for braving the repetitive push-button ringing of cash registers yet without access to the cash.

For each red and black rotation of the solar roulette of fortune, we wet our pants. The Sphinx of Toronto spumes chlorine gas from its anteater's snout; ever so mellifluently the poison infiltrates through human arteries while whole cities are evacuated from the complacency of snores and nightmares. Nerves fray like an extension of electric wires the likes of which the drowned priesthood of Atlantis could never have envisioned... in such fear like those three hours when the Leviathan's tracking screens went haywire deep in the belly of Cheyenne Mountain and fantasized renegade Behemoth missiles on the warpath. "Hear ye—ye true believers of the infamous exploits of Gargantua and Pantagruel— Rome had already proved for all eternity that there is no possible defense against the penetration of a mosquito's stiff proboscis," old Rabelais squealed.

Floating upon this these stormy asteroids, we have witnessed how Sputnik's mollusk spines titillated the martial spirits of ham radio operators, sending virus-loaded virilia into distant climes of the stratosphere. Irrespective of political salutations, scriveners now pore through military manuals to study the mirrors of Archimedes that once set aflame the fleet of Marcellus. (History is considered bunk only *after* the moment when the intrepid entrepreneur has come, seen, conquered.)

In the post-Sovieticus, phosphorescent Monitors and Merrimacs still battle it out like great sperm whales and giant squids, their missiles guided by flying computers. Melville's war has lost its glory to the mundane utilitarian mechanization of the gatling gun. Where is individual honor? Where chivalry? All history just rusts away until a split second of a blown fuse and collision of interplanetary space junk. All evolution is convoluted from a state of primordial menstruation, and ages to a purgatorial menopause. Who forged this brittle metal? Upon what dire anvil? With what dread gas? Exactly what was it you prophesied, beaming eyed Blake? Would the fires of Orc be stemmed? What of the Demon red with clouds?

Yet *Ye Olde Truth Book* responded NADA NADA NADA NADA NADA at the very moment when a twelfth century mullah had declared Holy War against all satanic whores and pimps. The conflict seemingly perpetual, the captors of Gulliver's children, after having once pretended to dump overpriced wines into the D.C. gutter, are now swarming on speedboats dropping Styrofoam floats before battleships directly below the next defecation of the Leviathan and its parasitic cowbirds that lay ever inflating multitrillion dollar turds on the odds of the already disastrous outcome. If still not convinced, then re-interpret the words of Nostradamus as so desired:

"Rain, famine, war in Persia having not ceased,
Too great a faith shall betray the Monarch.
The end planned and conceived in France,
A secret sign for one to be more sparing."

In other words, the messianic holocaust stewed from black gold (the putrid wine distilled in the ovaries of the earth and sipped in porcelain cups) was obviously prefabricated. [*Made in France.*] The semen of planned obsolescence had already been impregnated into the very architectonic design of the cosmic assembly line. It was naturally Nostradamus who foresaw how holy messages could be encrypted through Internet *steganography: But who?— the Leviathan?— is supposed to be "more sparing"?*

If still not believers, then regard the Congress of Vultures that hover above us in a cohesive pack upon spy satellites. Their sharpened talons clutch the multiple warheads of barbed missiles while waiting the moment to mobilize the call of the wild with their shrieks. Focus the zoom lens to observe the clenched fists in opposition that salute the aerial bombardment of saliva and rotten eggs... Let us thus not err, too wasted, into the bottomless pit that awaits us. Are we to believe? To determine whether this will be yet another Jonathan Edward's gospel sales pitch, a public promotion for a new book, or a premonition of a verifiable *TRUTH* will be, in itself, a millennial task...

In the distance, on the forgotten half of the planet, we spy in televised re-runs the golden hooves of Shisha-smoking Saracens and rebellious buzkashi players who once brought both Albion Redcoats and Muscovy Knights to their knees— after the Leviathan tricked the Soviet Behemoth into invasion with flying elephant gun ships bursting into flames stung by incendiary missiles. We claim we cannot comprehend the terror of stoning once our own home cooked barbeque escapades in rice paddies have fizzled out— in outrage against Buddhas of Bamiyan dynamited in idolatrous envy in ostensible protest against development assistance for statues— not the poor.

Impossible to measure on the Richter scale, that giant blast incites those prematurely prophesied riders of an apocryphal Apocalypse to saddle their white, red, black, pale horses in a hangman's posse of conquest, revenge, speculation, *TERROR...* The same Beasts provide a perfect pretext for the Timocratic Leviathan to dig itself deep into Mesopotamian quicksand in adulation of Jingoist Albion as it similarly wrestled the Sphinx and Sudanese Mahdi in blistering heat more than a century before. Regard Sura #18 "The Cave" for confirmation: *"On that day, when Gog and Magog are spoiling the land, we shall let some of them surge against others and the Trumpet will be blow."*

Thus so storm clouds continue to rage in pure fury in concealing killer nano-satellites that gyrate within our presence promoted by Von Braun rocketeers with solar powered batteries to appease those who are still enamored with the chimes of natural harmony. Yet to the dismay of these same self-righteous defenders of nature, one delinquent debutant after another flicks plutonium ashes into oceanic suds. Naturally these nouveau-riche members of the radiating jet set flirt flagrant promiscuity in high society gossip columns. (Watch as the planet's quintessential dietetic resource— plankton— is overspiced with scrumptiously irradiated flavors— *Zataar; Tandoori* or *Balti Masala; Kim-Chi;* with *Ghormeh-Sabzi* promoted on the way— a breakfast for tsunami champions and truly food for thought for the UN P-5 nuclear club!)

"To be bright as light, yet not to dazzle!" This ancient wisdom of Lao Tze is certainly not that of Pekinese Tarot players who once stammered clumsily railroading huge mobile packages into fixed indigo silos rotting with subsidized grain, but who now possess new laser versions of war-fighting video games with near real time vision. Not a soul has been enlightened: The softest things shall devour the hardest! The meek shall inherit!

If still not believers, then necessity dictates the abandonment of all idealist materialist romantic positivist prophetic theses! Even if Marx, resurgent, should claw out of his battered grave, who would recognize him? (History has sworn that he shall appear in the form of either Lazarus or Dracula upon listening to the miswired dialectics of dilettante computers, depending on the class perspective of optical illusions achieved in virtual reality.)

So what is the significance of history's oracles, which conceal themselves within hieroglyphics, upon cryptic rune stones, or that whisper from the lips of bog men frozen for all eternity in enigma? What do diviners say? Who will lead us to the Promised Land and promise likewise not to be struck down by the bullets of assassins?

With no response to our queries, heavenly assurances mass like prefabricated masonry troops housed for tourists in imperial tombstones, yet untrained for crowd control. As we press our bodies firmly against the catacomb walls of civil defense drills, we feel childhood lice festering in our scalps: Our hair leaps like the fur legs of centipedes to striped bandanas self-tied with a hangman's knot to our necks. Undetected by invaders outside the Great Wall, megalithic Fire Ravens, steeped in a kaleidoscopic poison, rise in unison (after tracing the mobile missile treads of the Behemoth) to proclaim blood wrath upon the vicissitudes of human evolution— in pinpointing the Beautiful Isle,

Okinawa, the satellites of stardom, Hollywood and L.A.'s Chinatown. All within circular t/error probability!!!

***

A shower of flaming arrows alights the sky like the sun behind the flight of geese... Flame throwers of smokeless fire, emerald swords and three-bladed javelins with swift-striking shafts triggered by sound waves flash through the haloed sky through what seems a hundred suns, a hundred moons, a myriad of stars... But then— no night... no day... all points of the compass utterly lost... the rain is black...

The clocks had stopped at 8:15. A metal lunch box filled with boiled peas and rice broiled from the inside. The bronze Buddha smelted at 7,000 degrees; glass bottles writhed like yellow serpents. A school uniform hung buttoned to a tree; the child's body was nowhere to be found. A glass lens glistened from the eye socket of a skull severed from its corpse. The flash had evaporated the paint from the walls, the shadows of the bodies remain frozen for all time.

A young girl smiled with a broad grin outside a window of a collapsed home surrounded in rubble. A solemn mother milked her baby whose face was scarred with deep burns. Warm winds approached from the distance; there were many small fires, as if set off by fireflies, smoldering. Those at ground zero had disappeared in a white flash without a trace; those at a distance could not understand what ever-burning horror had inserted itself beneath their leprous flesh. Hair dropped from their scalps just a few weeks later.

The pilot of the Enola Gay watched the towering flames of Little Boy from the clouds out of the pure blue heavens once the bomb had hit Hiroshima. The pilot of Bock's Car was supposed to have hit the arms factories and secret chemical weapons plants at Kokura, but on account of bad weather, he veered toward clearer skies and watched the blaze of Fat Man as it struck the city of Nagasaki. A third bomb was prepared to strike August 18. There had been plans to drop three a month in September, October,

November— and up to seven in December. Niigata and the imperial capital and sacred city of Kyōto had also been listed as potential targets. Years later, the pilot of the Enola Gay put it this way: "You hate to see them as collateral damage, but the weapon is non-selective. It has no discrimination. That's the way I look at it." His co-pilot cried, "My God, what have we done!" The pilot of Bock's Car never spoke publicly about it...

***

Blinded by the instant flash of shocking memories, we cannot observe the contenders for the throne, only the multitudes who tremble in supplication before a flame of far greater intensity than that sparked by the silicon chips Prometheus once stole. *Who then dare stand against the fissionable glitch of an eclipsed fuse?* Dare those of the Marx-Mayakovsky-Maoist Yue-fu Poet Bureau? Those of the Nietzsche-Pound-Mishima Unity&Order Cult? Those of elite Yeats-Eliot-Stevens aesthetic entropy? Or those of the poppy-smoking anemic anomie of the Coleridge-DeQuincey-Rimbaud Oriental Romantics Club? Or the booze-bored Li Bai(jiu)-Poe-Plath heresy? Indeed, upon which leaning Internet tower are all poets now babbling?

Upon re-entry into slums of urban pollution, our eyes glaze as if coated by varnish. For typically exorbitant fees, surgeons operate on the ocular nerves. Once the corneas are removed, smog becomes as transparent as crystalline waters. Truth serum injected, confessions are demanded upon the torture racks of penal colonies. The pins of acupuncture are now the devices of invisible inquisitors:

"What caused your blindness? From what are you here to be cured?... Upon careful examination, we have discovered no such disease recorded in our texts... For the time being, which sedative do you prefer?... Be faithful, and wait with patience. The research cannot drag on forever. Some prescription must always fill the blank."

—1980; 2008

Rival Doomsday Sects

I.

Grit flails the eyes
where I wince upon this park bench
in these days more like summer
than winter

and stare in sheer panic
at the knight's forked attack:
"Mere game plans" deem the annals
of common wisdom.

Yet it is these rival chess players,
both known and unknown,
who man the turrets and command
posts of this very odd season.

II.

Loneliness my guide,
I wander from museum of art
to art boutique:

Neon red sculptures glower
much like my electric heater;
my soul dehydrates.

I walk counter-current
against the direction of floor arrows
and retrace his steps in time.

K. is slouched over his desk tediously
filing worker's comp forms in his 'double life'
for the Kingdom of Bohemia.

At a younger age, he returns in shock
from the gymnasium and climbs
the spiraling lightless staircase:

The cook had nicknamed him 'Ravachol'—
the French Anarchist. K.'s overbearing father
freaks him out: He's "a criminal, a murderer."

That Sunday, K. dizzily regards
his three sisters, Elli, Valli, Ottla,
dressed in their finest outfits.

His bat-like ears pick up schoolgirl
chit-chat. Long curling ribbons
adorn their cherub faces...

His adrenaline hallucinates
nightmares of ink running
upon his neatly bleached shirts:

Visions of Exodus floating upon Rafts
of the Medusa: The Promised Land
in the blood of others begotten.

III.

Homemade apple cider
and Russian *borscht;*

matza balls and gefilte fish;
hummus, harissa and falafel:

All make strange bedfellows
in my digestive track.

Is co-habitation of the planet's
intestinal linings

still possible?
Or will rival amino acids

vaporize one another
in a final gastro-nuclear fart?

IV.

Shielded   by its armored plates
the Rhinoceros slouches forth!

The Battle of Sticks   commences
when it peers   behind the cover

of a limo's   tinted glass
confronted   by a throng of warriors

who are camouflaged   by self-carved
masks   and who wield   *NOTHING*

but bamboo sticks in their fury.
Their shrieks pierce the Heavens

before their sticks clatter
in splinters to the pavement.

This night yet another night
Mr. Human Rights sweeps the streets

of Humanity to pledge his traitorous
allegiance to the royal Beasts.

Only the trench coats are permitted
to slink behind the cover of verdure

to hand out the leftover dinner scraps
to the palms of their pawns.

Together these spies skulk
within the crowd waiting to ambush

those who sacrifice their
nakedness to omnipresent Eyes.

Yet before my eyes is yet another
of those Apparitions of that *OTHER*

which has oozed forth from its womb
mutated beyond all human proportion.

Indeed its arteries flush
black-gold through its crude hide

and its rabid jaws savor
the thighs of those it ensnares.

Who are they who will dare
resist the amoeboid regeneration

of its mutant kin? Who will dare
oppose the blunt tusk of its thrust???

V.

The day it snowed—
Barefoot toes rummaged through rubble:
Sticks... stones... became the toys of children.

The day it snowed—
Black shawled women roasted lamb
over funeral pyres before makeshift shacks.

The day it snowed—
An "X" glazed the crystal storefronts:
The rifle butt rapped at each door.

The day it snowed—
Bombs were implanted in cars,
flattened like unleavened bread.

The day it snowed—
Amputated limbs rose to defy
the Phantoms of Solomon.

The day it snowed—
Eden's oasis eutrophied
from the Jordan to the Dead Sea.

The day it snowed—
Icicle daggers splintered into metal
fragments on soil possessed— by frost.

VI.

Musical X-mas card blares without cessation.
"Jingle bells... jingle bells... jingle all the way,"
the tintinnabulation that so musically swells.
Indeed, an endless jingoist hangover.

I remember I had gulped down mouth burning
canopies of *harissa* spread thick by an Iraqi hand
overlooked by his snickering spymaster. It was
Christmas eve; I was too respectful to refuse.

These words have written themselves in a seat
marked reserved for *les mutilés de guerre.* There
is still space. Body bags (leftover from Saigon)
have only just begun to arrive on desert sands.

In my mouth an aspirin tablet— effervescent—
foams rabid. I spit out metro doors held open by
two young *taggeurs*—one *Black,* the other *Beur.*
In Big Apple imitation, they've made their mark.

Thousands jam into the Bastille, climbing trees,
standing upon bus stop shelters. Cymbals clang,
"Quelle connerie la guerre!!!" Jaurès forewarns
of the Balkans— assassinated once again.

VII.

A miniature coffin,
it is draped with a green flag
with a crescent moon center
and ported by a dozen pall bearers.

Four spiraling towers
overlord all points of the compass.
Glued to the back of a leaf,
it brushes against the back of my hand.

Cool geometry dances lyrical
with venomous urticating setae—
nettles of Rushdie/Nasrin blasphemies—
pale-faced human forms erased.

This saddle-back Saladin
eats the green leaves of trees raw,
marching the faithful to martyrdom
in honeyed veneer of holiness.

VIII.

Four riders of a non-programmed Armageddon/ Yawm al-Qayāmah set off upon quotidian routes from Logan, Newark and Dulles over American airspace.

AA Flight 11 and UA Flight 175 then veer from their expected trajectory and lunge, one after the other, into each of the 110 story 1,368 ft aluminum and steel lattice north and south towers of the World Trade Center with its 104 passenger elevators and 21,800 windows, with its elite venture capitalist interior-exterior designed view of 45 smoggy miles in every direction.

Not able to escape – thousands are broiled alive in the volcanic explosion of a supra-urban Mount Megiddo holocaust – "symbolic" victims of an unconventional war fought using conventional aircraft. The Twin Towers then crumble into dust, crashing upon the streets below, littering the city with clouds of asbestos gray. A third plane, AA Flight 77, slams into the Pentagon in the midst of its glory of pushin' top-secret pulp.

The fourth plane, UA Flight 93, explodes over an empty field near Shanksville, PA, after what was said to be a valiant struggle by the passengers to fight the hijackers armed with explosives somehow snuck onboard. Others say the Pentagon itself blew the plane out of the sky to prevent it from pinpointing yet another target.

Some say UA Flight 93 was headed toward Camp David; some say the White House; some say toward the Three Mile Island nuclear power plant; some say the target was Fort Detrick, center of four bio-hazard research centers. Some say our boys knew about the attack, but didn't know exactly when or where; others say they had no idea it was coming; a few say it was a conspiracy. It was almost the debate over Pearl Harbor all over again…

For the tabloids, the billowing smoke from the Twin Towers seems "to bring into focus the face of the Evil One complete with beard and horns and malignant expression." The caption queries: "What do you see in the picture?"

IX.

The millennium had passed.
Gargoyles and dragons howled in warning
from the stone walls of the Church.
But no trumpets sounded.

Pope Urban II could bear it no longer.
After nearly a century of famine
and earthquake and pestilence,
the foundations had yet to crack!

Hallelujah! The trumpet sounded forth—
The whole western world to wage Holy War!
The crusaders rushed forth gallantly:
Clouds of arrows blackened the skies

like swarms of locust (how biblical!).
Yet flaming sagebrush parboiled flesh
beneath cotte de mailles and armored suits:
The Cross snagged upon the Horns of Hattin.

The Infallible One later sought an alliance
with the Russians and Mongols against
the Saracens. No luck. Is Saint George
still available for military service?

And where the hell is Prester John?

X.

Must the repeated horror
of lash after heinous lash
unleash even greater Terror?

Must yet another Blitzkrieg propel
yet one more people into the Millennia
of unwarranted Diaspora?

Must the poet's
redundantly recycled
prophecy—

of some vengeful creature
lurid as the sun—
soon stalk our progeny?

Was it truly toward
Bethlehem where that *Rough Beast*
slouched to be born?

Claim and counter-claim,
what was once apparent is no longer—
A myriad of webs spins the Gyre.

XI.

Yes, I remember how
the Apocalyptic Apocrypha
of rival doomsday sects

were once inscribed
upon the not yet completed
entrance to the D.C. Metro

become a *sub-terranean* latrine.
Yes, it was, indeed, a strange sky,
clouds silken as an oyster tongue...

Those tattered souls arose,
and made their yellow "marks" before
falling back asleep, spread-eagled,

basking for long hours on the lawn
within a solar kiln— without revealing
any sign of fear or trepidation...

But unlike those D.C. street prophets
I cannot swallow whole
the uneasiness of yuletide zephyrs:

My belly bloated
in false pregnancy,
I crave the burnt heads of matchsticks

and shiver sleepless
in the un-upholstered back seat
of an abandoned Cadillac

for I have witnessed
the early awakening
of cherry blossoms

garroted by unexpected slush.
I now ache from the decaying enamel
of the world empire and tremble

before the overwhelming dialectics
of its extricated wisdom teeth.
In this mid-winter reprieve,

we become giddy school children,
flirtatious, yet frightened,
let off early in the wake of a bomb scare.

—from 1977 to 2003

Have Seen The World's Children

Have seen their bloated blowfish bellies,
their gills barely pumping
overturned upon the oil-smeared surface;

    Have seen them howling like stray mutts
    their teeth gnawing deep into teething rings
    of fleshless bones;

Have seen the love children of bitter wars,
castaways asleep on park benches,
who clasp the photo of an officer and his maid;

    Have seen them wailing like street cats
    for a scrap of lard tossed to the alley
    by dowagers of *noblesse oblige;*

Have seen the child refugees
who sail in skeletal rafts of the Medusa
in search of a shadow of America;

    Have seen their families poisoned
    in abandoned lots by the quicksilver toxin
    of our *Civilization;*

Have seen their limbs contorted,
packed like mutant rats in homes for orphans
speaking of parents who were mere phantasms;

Have seen the child warriors
with machetes in hand, ready to dismember
whatever poor soul treads in their path;

Have seen the naïve minds of pre-teens
bombasted by television previews
of an *Apocryphal Apocalypse;*

Have seen their crack/smack brains fried,
their body organs yanked from their guts
offered for sale on street corners;

Have seen youth jeering, throwing stones
at the lies of the adult world
then gunned down for daring to speak out...

Children! Our Children!!!

—1978/2000

About Hall Gardner

Hall Gardner's poems have been published in: *Chanticleer* (No. 15, October 2006); *Sheets for Men Only: An International Anthology of Poetry & Prose* (Dancing Ink Press, 2004); *Fire Readings* (Frank: Paris 1991); *Catalyst* (Fall 1989); *Working Cultures* (Spring 1984); the *Peace or Perish Crisis Anthology* (San Francisco, 1983); *Hoo-Doo 7* (1980); *The Unrealist* (1980); *Three Sisters* and *Saxifrage* (Georgetown University); *Sol* (Howard University); the *Colgate Portfolio* (Colgate University), plus dozens of poems in the *Paris Atlantic* in the decade 1990–2000 (American University of Paris); the *Washington Peace Center Newsletter* (throughout 1980); *Visions; Ultramarino,* among many others. Two of his poems likewise appeared on the website of *Poets Against the War* in 2003. The title poem, "The Wake-Up Blast," was requested for the e-book, *Poems for Madrid,* edited by Todd Swift in 2004. His short story *Laundromat Reflections (14th of July)* was first published in *The Paris Times*, No. 5, February 2006; the full-length story appeared on-line on the *Nthposition* web magazine in March 2006 (London), edited by Val Stevenson, along with a number of critical essays.

Hall Gardner is also author of *Averting Global War: Regional Challenges, Overextension and Options for American Strategy* (Palgrave, 2007); *American Global Strategy and the "War on Terrorism"* (Ashgate, 2005; 2007); *Dangerous Crossroads: Europe, Russia and the Future of NATO* (Praeger, 1997); *Surviving the Millennium: American Global Strategy, the Collapse of the Soviet Empire, and the Question of Peace* (Praeger, 1994), among many articles (or chapters in his edited books) on international politics, global security issues and conflict resolution.

He is a professor at the American University of Paris.

E-mail: hall.gardner@aup.fr

www.ingramcontent.com/pod-product-compliance
Lightning Source LLC
Chambersburg PA
CBHW032051150426
43194CB00006B/491
9780615219561